To

my beautiful wife

Kay Elizabeth

who is one of a kind

and second in love only to my
Lord.

Acknowledgments

A huge thank You to the Lord for making this book possible.

To my dear wife, Kay, for her invaluable input, love, patience, and support.

I am immensely grateful to Pastor Donald Sheley from Church of the Highlands, San Bruno, California, USA, for co-authoring this book and for encouraging me to put pen to paper and write all these miracles and challenging experiences to help inspire and build up the body of Christ.

A huge thank you to the many friends and co-workers in the ministry here in Borneo and elsewhere in the world for their marvelous input to bring the vision of this place to reality. And thank you to many others who in whatever way, have helped to get this book edited, published, and printed.

Ronny Heyboer

Foreword

There are some experiences in life that are simply unforgettable. They leave you breathless. Words fail to describe how you feel. Days, weeks, and years go by, but the scene never fades from your mind.

For me, it was late at night in the jungles of Borneo. The journey from the border of Malaysia had been long and difficult. Deep potholes filled the roads, making the ride bumpy and uncomfortable. I prayed that we soon would reach our destination … Living Waters Village. And then it happened.

In the distance, we caught our first glimpse of street lights. Impossible! A *city* in the middle of the jungle?! It's a scene I would never forget. Awaiting us was a man whom I had heard so much about but never met. His name: Ronny Heyboer.

Read his story, feel his passion, learn about his dream that has become a staggering reality: A children's village for 1,000 children in crisis, a medical center, school buildings to accommodate 2,000 children, and living quarters to house all the children and staff. I must admit, it was a concept I first thought impossible. But miracles do happen! And when you finish reading this book, I am sure you will be breathless, too.

God bless you!
Pastor Donald Sheley

Index

An Encounter with "White Man"

The bugs went into hiding, the rats were all sleeping, so my hunt for food that day left me with an empty stomach. You see, my daily diet was limited to the animals and the bugs of the jungle.

My name is Ezra. I was only six years old then, but life had been difficult already. Mother died when I was four years old. Father died a few months later. I was alone and there was no one to care for me. In my village, located deep in the jungles of Borneo, everyone was poor. Each person had to search for his own food. Many died of starvation. Nobody wanted me because I was just one more mouth to feed.

My little body was wasting away. Scabies crawled beneath my skin, tuberculosis was rotting away my lungs, and I was suffering from severe malnutrition.

It was time to return to my rickety chicken coop for the day was almost over. The chicken coop was my protection from the daily rains. Crawling under the thick jungle undergrowth, I had to cross a small stream before reaching the village. Then I spotted a White Man bathing in the crystal clear water running down from the mountains.

I had been told that if I didn't obey my parents, they would turn me over to the White Man. Still, I did not fear him. He had visited our village before so I approached him. He offered me his hand – I don't know why, but I felt perhaps I could trust this man; he might be different, he might even care... He took me to the hut of our tribal chief.

After greeting the chief, he asked who I belonged to and who was responsible for me. The chief replied, “His father and mother are dead. He’s on his own. We don’t want him.”

“Then can I take him with me back to my village?” asked the White Man. “I’ll take care of him. But he will live with me, and I will not return him to this village.”

The White Man really wanted me. He said that he would care for me and feed me. My little heart leapt for joy!

After a brief conversation with the chief, it was agreed that I could go. To this day, I still remember the words of my chief, “Take him. We do not want him.”

I had no clothes except for the dirty, ragged shorts I had on. The White Man picked me up and hugged me. We started toward his car. I had never ridden in a car, and everything seemed weird to me. The sound of the engine frightened me, but the White Man touched my hand and told me everything would be all right. My native tribal dialect was a different language from his, so our conversation was very limited. But I felt that he loved me, so my mind was at peace.

After a long journey, we arrived at a building

that he said was his house. What an odd building – with doors, windows, floors, and chairs to sit on! This was so different from my chicken coop. I visited each room; each had different furniture. Some rooms that the White Man called bedrooms had beds, with sheets on them. Then there was a room he called the toilet. He showed me how it worked. Never had I sat on a chair with a hole in it, and after pushing the lever, the bowl filled with water, and then the water disappeared! It was so strange.

Soon after I arrived, my new family members served me a plate of food. I was so hungry that I grabbed the rice and stuffed it into my mouth. Guarding my plate to make sure that no one took it away, I ate every last morsel. It was so good! To eat from a flat plate was different because in the jungle, a leaf from the nearby tree served as our plate.

The White Man took me to a man whom he called a doctor. The only doctor I knew was the witchdoctor in our village. I feared the witchdoctor and obeyed his every word. But this doctor was different. He was kind.

After the doctor looked at every part of my body, he told the White Man that I was suffering from extreme malnutrition, tuberculosis, and scabies. Then he said to my newfound friend, "If you had not brought this child today, he would be dead in one week."

With our hands full of medicine bottles, we returned to my new home. Because my body was so

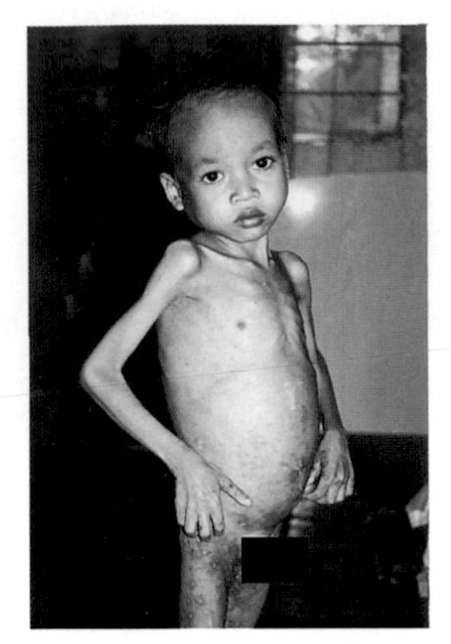

Left: *Ezra when we found him in the jungle on July 27, 1991. Looking at his teeth and fine motor skills, we guessed he must have been around six years old. The date we found him is now his birthday.*
Right: *Ezra six months later. His skin is cleared from scabies, his body is worm free, his eyes are bright and glowing, his hair is growing and shining. He has no more nightmares and a giant smile.*

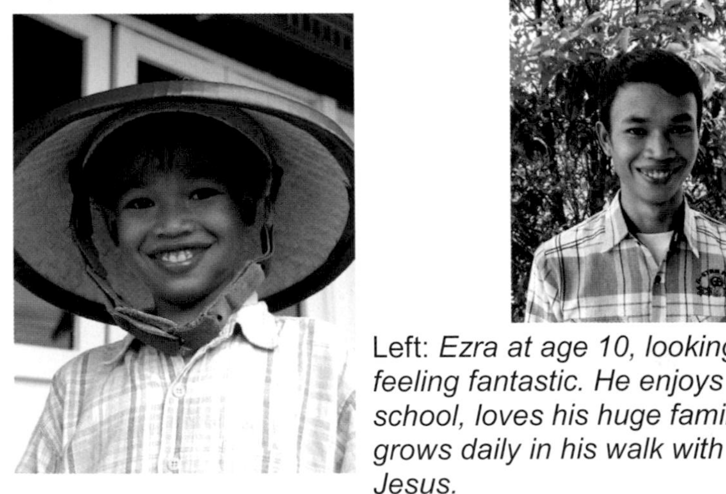

Left: *Ezra at age 10, looking and feeling fantastic. He enjoys school, loves his huge family, and grows daily in his walk with Jesus.*
Right: *Ezra now in his senior years of high school.*

The day Ezra met his brother, Arip, for the first time, after many years of thinking he was dead. That day Ezra was the happiest child in the world. Arip was overwhelmed. His emotional and physical scars were evidence of a harsh life in the jungle without parents or anyone to care for him.

Ezra and Arip now. Both are great young men, so happy and grateful to the Lord for abruptly changing the course of their lives, from utter hopelessness to a life of victory in Jesus.

Below: *The three musketeers. Jefri, Joel and Ezra. Friends forever!*

sick, the doctor instructed my friend that the food portions should be very small, and that I should be fed several times a day.

Soon, my tummy began to get bigger and healthier. I felt happy and safe. And after a few weeks, the scabies were gone and my skin felt so soft. My hair began to grow, black and shiny. After six or eight months, my little body looked healthy, and I felt well.

The White Man had become my father. I called him "bapak," Indonesian for "dad." One day I told Bapak I had an older brother, Arip, who was lost in the jungle. I wanted him to be with me. Bapak suggested that he go visit the village and see if he could find Arip and bring him to our home. When he arrived at the village, Bapak asked the chief if he knew where he might find my brother. The chief said he was somewhere in the jungle, looking for food. Bapak waited a long time. Finally, it began to get dark so he left for home. On three different occasions, Bapak visited the village and was told each time that Arip was somewhere in the jungle looking for food. Bapak thought this was their way of telling us that he was dead.

A few years later, one of my new older brothers, named Antan who lived in our home decided he would go to his village. It is located half an hour from my village. It also belonged to our tribe, called the Matee tribe. He wanted to visit his mum and brothers. As he was looking for food in the jungle for the family one day he came across Arip who was also looking for food! Antan couldn't believe his eyes. He embraced Arip and told him we had searched for him many times but thought he was dead. After obtaining permission from the chief, they left together for our home.

Life in my new home with Bapak was wonderful. We ate three times a day, we slept in comfortable beds with sheets, and we were learning about Jesus. Soon my brother, Arip, and I received Jesus into our lives, and we started our education in one of the local schools.

That was all in the past. Today, I am a senior in high school. My brother is now busy in the activities and work responsibilities at Living Waters Village.

I often think back to that scene in the river, seeing that strange White Man taking a bath. How I thank God that our paths crossed that day! To me, he was like an angel of God, sent to this wild jungle. He took me, a starving six-year-old, and loved me, fed me, and helped to heal me. Even today, Bapak is still caring for me.

Living on Two Continents

My name is Ronny Heyboer. I was born in the town of Wangaratta in Victoria, Australia, to parents who weren't particularly well off. In 1955, my parents migrated from Holland to Australia, and life had not been that good in their newly chosen country. Over the years Dad worked in general labour projects, doing whatever he could to feed his wife and three sons.

As young boys, we did not know we were not well off. Wherever we lived, however, Mum made it home, even though there were times we lived in places that were tough going. I remember that we lived in a cow stable on a tobacco farm for a time where Dad and Mum found seasonal work. The stable was very small with no door or windows but mum hung some curtains around to give us some privacy and she always had the gift of making nothing into something homely. I recall her saying to me then that it didn't matter if we went through difficult times like this because later on, when life is a bit kinder to us and we had more things to enjoy, we would appreciate what we had then. I have never forgotten those words and I have always, until this day, thanked the Lord for even the little things that most of us take for granted, like water, electricity, a fridge, and even a clean toilet with toilet paper. What a blessing. Can you imagine life without these things?

My father was always busy looking for work or doing work. He was a good dad who loved and cared for us but because he wasn't around much, I didn't get to know him very well. It wasn't until I was married and had my own children that I got to know my dad well.

My brothers and I liked the wide open spaces of Australia, and we could always find a place to run, a tree to climb, or a stream to fish or swim in. Our school near the cow stable was very small, just a dozen or so students, all in one room. We had one teacher for the whole primary school. There were two kids in grade one, one kid in grade two, none in grade three, three in grade four, etc. It was great. Many times we would go outside and have our lessons under a tree, or up the tree, or while fishing in the creek. When the teacher was unavailable, or had to move for whatever reason, we had to be bussed into the nearest town. That was an adventure every day because the bus was very old and would often break down. As a result, we would usually be very late arriving at school. I didn't mind because the town schools were boring compared to our country school.

Life was difficult for my family in many ways. Dad received news from Holland that his mother was very ill and possibly dying. My grandfather had already died the year before. Dad wanted to go back to Holland before Grandma died. However, the other reason, the *real* reason for wanting to go back to Holland, was kept secret from us for many years.

Mum and Dad's marriage was on the rocks. The tension in the home was beginning to take its toll on the marriage, and the constant shortage of funds to support the family made the decision to leave very easy. Tickets were purchased from the sale of the commission house Dad had bought a number of years before. In those days, the government wanted everybody to be able to own their own house and made it possible with cheap government loans. Ordinary hard working folks could then buy their home instead of throwing money away each week on rent. But because Dad could no longer find work and therefore couldn't pay off the loan, he decided to rent our house to someone who did have a job and could pay rent. Dad could continue to pay the loan off with the rent money while we moved from place to place wherever he could find work.

With our tickets in hand, we boarded the big ship, the *Achille Lauro*. We were on our way to Holland with the few belongings we possessed. I was eight years old. Although it was exciting to board such a giant ship, I didn't want to leave Australia. I didn't want to go to Holland because I didn't want to live in a windmill and wear funny wooden shoes. Little did I know that Holland was not quite the same as the pictures portrayed in books. I loved my Australia and my boyhood memories meant so much to me. It was painful to leave my friends. I decided then that when I turned 18, I would return to Australia.

We spent five weeks on the ship. My brothers and I had fun running on the ship from stern to stem. We sailed through the Suez Canal, and into the Mediterranean Sea. We sailed past the Rock of Gibraltar and into the Atlantic Ocean. Our ship entered into a very severe storm along the coast of Portugal. Everyone was frightened and sick. My dad, having worked on the *New Amsterdam* liner for years, comforted us by saying that the storm wasn't that bad, and all would be fine. He said it would be considered dangerous and threatening if the crew came to seal the portholes with steel plates and bolts. He had barely finished his comment when there was a knock on the door of our cabin. Sailors came in and told us that the captain had ordered that all the portholes were to be sealed, and every precaution was to be taken for the worst. Now Dad was frightened and worried too. We rehearsed what to do if the ship sank, and waited for the storm to pass. After many terrible and sickening days, the waters calmed. The ship was severely damaged and needed urgent repairs.

We arrived at the port of Rotterdam in the winter of 1966. We had never seen snow, and the winds were freezing cold. We were greeted by our grandparents and other relatives, and it was decided that we would stay with our maternal grandparents until Dad found work and we could afford a place to rent.

Soon my father found a job, but tensions in the

marriage were becoming obvious to my brothers and me. Dad found extra work to try to improve our living standard, so he wasn't around much; and when he was around, he was always tired and grumpy, and gave us little attention. As I have already mentioned, I really did not know my dad. Although we were a part of the Catholic Church, religion was seldom discussed in our home. God was not mentioned. We went to church every week like everyone else we knew, since that was the traditional thing to do.

Thinking back to my school days in Australia, I attended a Catholic school for a brief period of time. Two people really impressed me because they were always talking about Jesus. It was Father Burns and a nun whose name I can't remember now. They loved Jesus so much. Although their talk and love for Jesus didn't impress me then, I often thought back years later to those godly people as I began my search for God.

I remember vividly one day at school when we had to go to church for confession; each child had to take turns to go into the confession box and confess their sins to the priest. When it was my turn, I told my teacher I didn't need to go because I had nothing to confess. She gave me a horrified look, and pointed to "the box." I realized I had better go or else there would be trouble. What do you confess when you have nothing to confess? I decided to make up a few things so that everybody would be pleased. So I told the priest that I had lied to my mother, broken a window somewhere, and stolen a few lollies. The priest told me to repent and not to do it again, and instructed me to say a few prayers. When I walked out of the box I remember standing still for a moment and thinking, *now* I do have something to confess. I just lied - but I was too embarrassed to go back.

After arriving in Holland, my parents enrolled my brother and me in the local school. We learned the Dutch language quickly, especially the swear words, which horrified our parents. We didn't realize they were swear words. I did not like it in Holland. To me it seemed like a concrete jungle everywhere and you were not allowed to do much. Everything was so controlled. You had to have a license for everything. In Australia we were free and nobody bothered us. We could go camping and fishing anywhere, swim anywhere, build a tree house anywhere, and even dig a hole if we wanted - and all for free! However, in Holland, nothing seemed free. If you wanted to fish, you had to apply for a license. If you wanted to build a tree house or dig a hole to make a cubby house in which to play, permission was required. You even had to pay to go swimming somewhere. The way I looked at it you had to have a license for everything. You almost had to have a license to pick your nose! I didn't like it there and I wanted to go home to my Australia. I was really homesick, and many times I dreamed of going back to my childhood home.

After six months or so, Dad found better work

at the Philips factory in Eindhoven. Philips also provided for a brand new rented house where we lived for many years. It had an extra bedroom that my parents eventually rented out to an Australian man who worked in the same company as Dad. At first, he seemed to be a very thoughtful and kind man, and we got along well. He gave special attention to me, but soon his behavior frightened me. He succeeded several times in touching the private parts of my body. I was too scared to tell my parents, so I kept it to myself and tried to resist his behavior. I started to dislike him and thought this was quite obvious to all, since first I used to get on so well with him and later I loathed him and didn't want anything to do with him. However, my parents didn't seem to notice, so it wasn't dealt with.

Until one day, when my Dad approached me and asked me if this guy had ever touched me where he shouldn't have. The question startled me. I remember telling my dad that this guy tried many times but never succeeded. That was a lie. I couldn't possibly own up that he did succeed. That would bring shame, dishonor, and disgust to the family. Dad asked the question because he found out that this guy had been violating a child in the neighbourhood. I was shocked at this news. Suddenly I realized it happened because of me: if I had told my parents the first time it happened, then this guy would have been dealt with and would not have messed with the other child. I felt so terribly guilty and still do in some way until this very day. I should have opened my mouth. I should have blown the whistle. I felt responsible for what happened to him. But it was too late. It didn't occur to me that the guy would go after someone else, but I was naïve concerning these matters. So many times people sweep these sorts of things under the carpet, keeping quiet so nobody will know or find out or get hurt. The truth is that it will never go away until it has been dealt with. Dad didn't take the matter to the police. At that time it wasn't the thing to do in such incidents. Instead he asked a doctor for advice. I am not sure what the doctor said, but my father told the offender to leave our house immediately and find somewhere else to live. Months later, I saw an ad in the paper: Some guy from Australia who loved children was looking for a place to stay. I could not help but think that this was him, probably caught again and looking for another house and another victim.

Many years later, when I became a Christian, I apologized to Dad and the other victim, now an adult, for not blowing the whistle then. How good it felt to have done that. Of course the memory and the pain are still there, but God helps us heal and then perhaps help other people who are going through similar experiences.

Life in our family was beginning to unravel. The man next door became attracted to my mother. Soon after, she decided to divorce my father. It was a scandal that rocked the family and shocked the neighbours, for this was the first divorce that the family and neighbourhood had to face. The guy had a wife and four children still living next door to us which created all sorts of bizarre situations and causing a terrible mess. You see, my father loved my mother and the divorce was unwarranted other than that they were not really suited for each other, but what could he do? My dad broke emotionally and couldn't cope with this turn of events in his life. He ended up going to a rest home where he was treated with antidepressants. When he returned home, he was told again that he had a few days to permanently leave the house so that our neighbour could move in. I remember that day. I was sitting on the couch in the lounge room, staring out the front window thinking about all that was going on. My father approached me and told me that my mother wanted a divorce. He would have to leave. Dad began to cry. I had never seen my father cry before. He put his head on my lap and cried uncontrollably. I didn't know what to do. I didn't know Dad. I had no relationship with him because he was never home, or at least it seemed that way. I remember feeling so embarrassed, angry, hurt, and totally confused. I didn't want to touch him and yet everything in me was telling me to hug him. But I never did. How I regret that to this day.

After leaving the family home, he found a small room in a boarding house across town. My brothers and I would visit him occasionally. A few years later, Dad met a lovely lady whose husband had died of cancer. She had two beautiful children whom I now consider my brother and sister. I don't believe in stepbrothers or half-brothers. I believe you are either a part of the family or you're not. So many families are riddled with problems because they don't see each other as equals. What a sad waste of valuable time, when life is so short. I remember when Dad invited us boys to meet his newfound friend. Although it seemed odd to see my dad with another woman, it felt good to see Dad happy again. Sari was a lovely lady and loved the Lord. She is the best thing that happened to my father. They eventually married and lived happily ever after.

Not only did the divorce destroy our home, it had a crushing effect on my life and on my brothers' lives. I was angry at God and wondered if He was really there, because if He was, then why was this happening in my family? Didn't He care for us anymore? I decided then that God probably didn't exist. It was best for me not to believe in anything. I started to dislike people and figured that people only hurt you. I decided that when I grew up I would go live on a deserted island somewhere. I could live alone so that no one could hurt me anymore. Of course I probably would have lasted only a day. I have learned since, of course, that we all need each other. We were created by God so that we could have an intimate relationship with Him, but also so that we can be there for one another, helping and caring for each other, encouraging one another and building each other up.

Life became so empty and confusing. Nothing

mattered anymore. I hated school and tried all sorts of ways to avoid it. If I did go to school, a problem would always send me to the principal's office. At the age of 16, I was told to leave the school and never to return. In other words, I was kicked out of school. I didn't care.

Not far from our home was a supermarket. I applied for a job with the manager. "Well," he said, "the only job I have is straightening up the empty bottles in the bottle room that have been placed there when returned by the customers." "Great," I said, "I'll take it." The bottle room was the worst work place. Everything was disorganized. It was total chaos. Four people had to collect empty bottles from the customers and sort them out in their respective crates and pallets. It took me a few hours to work out their primitive system. In a few days, I had the entire department cleaned up, sorted out, and set up so that one person could manage the entire room. The boss couldn't believe his eyes when he saw what was accomplished in such a short time. Needless to say he was very pleased. In fact, my manager was so impressed he gave me other assignments in the store. Soon he promoted me. I became the youngest floor manager ever in that supermarket chain. Unfortunately, this made the other employees jealous. They thought that I was after their jobs. Actually, all I wanted was to work for my wages and to please my boss.

As the months went, my employer, Bert, began

to treat me as a good friend and even like his own son. Frequently, he and his wife, Aaltje, and their two children would invite me to dinner at their house, which was next door to the supermarket. I became a part of their family at a time when I didn't feel like I had any family. Don't get me wrong. I loved my mum and I loved my dad, but home wasn't home anymore. I used to stay with Bert and Aaltje for days and nights, and thoroughly enjoyed their family life. At that time, I was renting a room from a man who rented out all his rooms to mainly university students. I got along reasonably well with all the occupants. Still, I often felt terribly lonely, and I would stay at Bert and Aaltje's place. One evening, I told them that I appreciated my job with them and all the training that they were giving me, but they needed to know that when I turned 18 years old, I was going home to Australia. They tried, but failed to change my mind. No one was going to stop me from returning home.

As a teenager, I used to have so many dreams of finally arriving in Australia. As I walked off the boat plank, I would see my cousins (with whom I used to play when I was little) in the distance. I got so excited that I started to run toward them, but it seemed the harder I tried to run the slower I was going. Just as I was ready to embrace them, my mother would wake me up telling me to get ready for school. I used to get so upset with her because I was almost where I wanted to be when she had awakened me at just the wrong time. I would be upset all day when that happened. It wasn't long before I had the funds to purchase my ticket on a big ship called *The Australis* sailing for Melbourne, Australia. It was a very happy day for me. Finally, I could leave all the pain and frustration behind me and start life all over again.

After five weeks on the boat I finally touched down on Australian soil in the port of Melbourne. I felt like the happiest person in the world! I was so excited that I wanted to kiss the ground when I got off the boat, just like the Pope does when he arrives in a country.

Although I was thrilled to be home again in Australia where people seemed so incredibly friendly and where life was so relaxed and enjoyable, things were not as I had imagined. Things had changed after ten years. In addition, I was homesick for my adopted family from the supermarket. Three months passed slowly. I purchased a plane ticket and flew back to Holland. You see, I was only 18 years old, and terribly confused in mind and heart. I had no home, a broken family, and now I was torn between two countries. Even on the flight, I was thinking how stupid I was. After all these years of resenting life in Holland, why did I ever decide to return there after only three months? I made the decision, right there and then on the plane, to get a job quickly and save my money so I could get back to Australia as soon as possible. Pretty mixed up!

Back in Holland, I immediately returned to my adopted family. In moments, I had a job and I had a family who loved me as their son. Meanwhile, my mother seemed happy living with Jos, our former neighbour. His wife and kids had moved away which made things a little more "normal" so to speak. Jos is a great guy and the two of them could not live without each other. I learned to respect and admire him, and sometimes even call him Dad because of his love for us. It wasn't always like that. I left home when I was 17 because he used to drink a lot. We could never have a decent conversation without him talking about things that made me uncomfortable. I told my mother then that I didn't want to live with a drunk. *She* had chosen him, not me. She was very upset but understood and eventually gave him an ultimatum - stop drinking or get out. Thankfully, he chose the former. He changed so much. I am so grateful that he did. You couldn't find a better person now.

But back then, I was still restless. Where was God? Was He really out there somewhere? If God really existed, why did He let my family fall apart? My mind struggled with these questions frequently, especially at night.

After almost a year in Holland I flew back to Australia. Exactly where would I go? How long would I be there? I didn't know. I just knew I was going somewhere.

My Quest for God

At the age of 19, I returned to Australia to find a tight job market. Wages were minimal, and many were out of work. But I learned that one of the local grocery stores was looking for help so I applied, having had supermarket experience.

The man in charge was very specific, "If you come to work in my store, you must wear a tie."

"But I don't wear ties," I said. "Never have and never will."

"Then you can wear a scarf," he suggested.

"No," I insisted, "I won't wear a scarf either."

His response: "No tie, no scarf, no job!"

"Fine with me," I said, and I left.

When I arrived back at my uncle's house, he couldn't believe his ears. "You idiot," he said. "Jobs are scarce, and you turned down a good job because you won't wear a tie? People look for a job for months. You find one in just a few days, and you won't wear a tie?" I assured him that I would find work soon.

Then I heard a local cleaning service was looking for someone to wash windows, vacuum floors, and empty garbage in the office buildings and pubs that it was servicing. I applied, got the job, and I vacuumed floors, washed windows, and emptied garbage for one year. The job paid a decent salary, and I learned a lot. But all the time I was wrestling in my mind about this whole idea of God. Is there a

God? How do I find Him? I've heard about Jesus, but is there someone higher than Him?

But there was another matter that filled my thought life as well. I wanted to get married and have many children. When I was in the fourth grade in Holland, there was a girl who always participated in the skits we performed in the drama class. She liked me, and I felt the same about her. But years had gone by since we last talked. Before leaving for Australia, I met that same girl. She was then 17 years of age, pregnant, and on her way to America to marry a Texan. It was so good to see her again, but such a shame it was so brief. A few years later, when I had already settled in Australia, she wrote to me saying she was back in Holland with her little daughter. Her husband had left her for another woman, so she divorced him. We corresponded regularly and started to build a relationship. Eventually, we decided that she and her daughter should come to Australia. Soon Berty and her beautiful three-year-old, Tanja, joined me in Australia. Shortly after they arrived, we decided to get married in the Catholic Church, following our family tradition. Although we neither knew God, nor had a relationship with Him, we did want Him to be our witness.

Life after marriage continued in Australia. Besides working as a cleaner, I also found employment on a farm, mixing grain to feed thousands of cattle. My next job was working in a textile factory, which was a great challenge for me. I learned many skills there, particularly working with different people from different backgrounds with many different problems. Over the years, various job experiences would prepare me for what was ahead. Little did I know then what was to come.

Married life had its joys, and my job was bringing me good success, but my heart was still empty. I so wanted to know if God was real, and if He was, then how does one get to know Him? So one day, I decided to make a deal with this God that I wasn't sure existed. I spoke out loud, although I made sure that nobody was around to hear me, "God, if You really exist, then You must in some way reveal Yourself to me. I must know the meaning of life. I remember learning at school a long time ago about Jesus, but that's all. I need to know that You are for real. I will make a promise to You: I will go and buy a Bible and I will read it from cover to cover, even the boring bits I will read. But by the time I have read the last page, You must have revealed Yourself to me. Otherwise that's it, You've had Your chance with me. I will then go somewhere else."

A few days later, I went to a Christian book shop. "Do you have a Bible?" I asked. To my amazement, the shopkeeper pointed to a huge wall full of Bibles of all shapes and sizes. I asked for the cheapest one. I didn't want to spend too much money on a book. Months later, I realized that the Bible I bought was a Catholic Bible. I didn't know there were different versions.

I remember several years later when I was in Bible College, one of our lecturers was sharing about Shadrach, Meshach, and Abednego, who did not bow down to Nebuchadnezzar. When he threatened to throw them into the furnace, they still refused to obey. I was fascinated with the story. I raised my hand, commenting that it was just like the other story with King Nebuchadnezzar that I had read about. Here's that other story: A mother with seven sons stood in front of the king. They were ordered to bow down to him, or else he would execute each son, one at a time in front of all the others, including the mother. Their mother encouraged them by saying in her own language not to listen to this brute and never bow down to anyone but God, even if they were tortured to death. God would reward them. One by one, they were executed as each one refused to bow down. After each execution, the mother would encourage the others not to give in and bow down, but to stay focused on God.

My lecturer was baffled. He said that such a story was not in the Bible. I argued that it was. I couldn't have made up a story like that even if I tried. Of course it was in the Bible. Yet he insisted it was not in the Bible.

I couldn't understand why a teacher in a Bible College didn't know the Bible himself. I was pretty annoyed. At home I told my wife what had happened in the classroom. She, too, looked perplexed and said, "He is right, that's not in the Bible!" Now I was really confused. I didn't know the lecturer that well, but I knew my wife, and when she said that it wasn't in the Bible, then it probably wasn't. But how could that be? I was really confused and tried to find it in my Bible.

The next day she said to me, "I think it may be in your first Bible, the Catholic Bible, which includes 12 extra books called the Apocrypha books." Indeed, this was the case. When I approached my lecturer again the next day, I told him that he was right. The story wasn't in his Bible, but I was right too as it was written in the Catholic Bible, my first Bible. He smiled and gave a sigh of relief.

Returning to the story of my promise to God, I started to read the Bible at work, where I was a weaver looking after many weaving machines. I also cleaned dishes and served people at a local Chinese restaurant several nights a week. So I didn't have much free time to read. Each coffee break or lunch break, everyone would go outside for a smoke or whatever, but I grabbed my Bible. As I started from Genesis, the words just came alive. They penetrated deep into my mind and my heart as if they were speaking directly to me. I was so excited, but also shaken by what I was reading and how it was having an effect on me. I couldn't get enough of it. I had to read and keep on reading. I was so absorbed in reading. Maybe this God was talking to me! My coffee and lunch breaks were very short, and they just zoomed by when I was buried in the Bible. I remember one day, I realized that I was such a sinner who was not worthy to even read this book. It took me a long time to figure out that there was a way to have your sins forgiven through Jesus Christ, but I only understood that much later.

One day during a rest period, I was interrupted by one of my co-workers. He stopped and stared at me with a puzzled look. He asked what I was reading. I thought to myself, "He already knows what I am reading but just wants to show his disapproval." I told him I was reading the Bible, and I didn't care what he thought.

"Reading the Bible is great," he replied. "I have never seen anybody here ever read the Bible."

Then he asked, "When did you get saved?"

"Saved from what?" I answered.

"I mean when did you become a Christian?"

"I'm not," I replied. "I am simply reading this book. Can't I?" I asked a bit sarcastically because I thought he was still having a go at me.

He asked if I went to church and I replied that I didn't. He still looked puzzled. He invited me to his home group on Wednesday evenings. I wanted to know what it was. He simply replied, "Oh, we have some Bible studies, sing a few songs, pray, and have fellowship together." It all sounded strange to me, but there was something about this guy. When he said they had Bible studies I was interested. I wanted so desperately to know a lot of things that I didn't understand. Each time I read the Bible, words or sentences would pop up at me. I would write a question mark next to the passage, and underline the words. I would ask God, if He were there, please explain this to me. I would tell God that what I had just read didn't make any sense at all. "Please Lord, explain!" When I arrived home from work, I told my wife what had happened and asked her if she would like to come to this home group as well. Although very reluctant, she agreed to attend with me.

We got to the meeting late and encountered a strange sight. People were raising their hands and singing hallelujah songs with such passion. We looked at each other and could hardly contain our laughter. We are definitely in the wrong place here, we thought. This is obviously one of those cults people often talk about. It was all very funny to us. We didn't want to offend anyone, so we decided to sit down and stay to the end of the meeting. After the singing came the Bible study. It was fascinating, yet baffling. You see, during the study, they were answering my questions - the very ones I had marked in my Bible. How could they know that? That is not a coincidence. I thought it was a setup. Someone, obviously the guy I met at work, had looked into my Bible and saw those question marks. That's obviously one of the ways they lure their prey into this cult, I thought. But I am not that stupid. They don't know who they're dealing with. I will not fall for that. And it certainly was a setup, I would later conclude: not by man, but by God. Prayer followed and then fellowship. It was this fellowship time that really grabbed my heart. These people from all ages and cultures seemed so sincere in caring for each other. Some were cooking meals for people in need each day - people who weren't even one of them. Young people were coordinating which old people's lawns they would mow that week to bless them. Others were gathering funds to send to missionaries serving the Lord in different countries. I didn't know what missionaries were! People were so kind, friendly, and so genuine. They had something I didn't have. They seemed to have a love for one another that was foreign to me. I thought that either these people are popping happy pills each morning to be like this, or they truly have met with God who has changed them. I knew I had to come back. I wanted to know more. I wanted what they had.

When we arrived home, my wife was adamant. "I'm not going back there again. Those people are crazy!" And she was firm. My response, however, was different. I didn't understand much of what had taken place, but the following Wednesday I was at the meeting again. On my fourth visit, I was convinced that these people really knew the God I was searching for, so I asked them to help me pray. That night a total transformation took place in my mind and my heart. The empty feeling was gone. Joy and love abounded in my heart, and my Bible became so easy to understand! At age 26, my quest for God was finally over. I'd found Him! My life was turned upside down: no more drinking, swearing, or smoking. I wanted nothing to do with what I thought was sinful. I became radical for God, I mean *really* radical. I couldn't stop talking about Jesus. I so wanted my wife to experience what I was experiencing. Yet the more I talked to her about Jesus, the more she became hostile toward Him and me in every way. Instead of encouraging her and being patient, my criticism of her and her lifestyle was a constant irritant in our marriage and our home. It seemed that our lives – and our family - were being pulled apart in opposite directions.

My wife felt that she had lost the man she married. She became angry with the people who had introduced me to this religious experience and the God with whom I had fallen in love. Eventually, it created such a strain in our marriage that we became two separate people. Intimacy in our marriage ended; housekeeping chores were avoided. She would spend most evenings with her friends in the pub, at their place, or back at our place. Sometimes she would stay out all night, and I wouldn't know where she was. I didn't know if she was having an affair, or if the car was wrapped around a tree somewhere. When I asked her where she had been, she would tell me in many colorful words to mind my own business. This situation went on year after year. Frequently, my anger would produce fits of rage that destroyed my Christian testimony to my wife. "And you call yourself a Christian," she retorted. "You are all loonies." I would get mad at myself. In my anger, I failed to be a good witness. My nights were often spent crying and praying, asking God to do something to save our marriage. I knew the pain of divorce and that was the last thing I wanted to happen. Some people suggested that I should get a divorce because this was no life I was leading. I would respond by saying that I would keep my marriage vows to love and care for her, "in good times and in bad times." Well, this was a bad time, and I had made a promise.

However, during those first four years of being a Christian, the joy was slowly being sucked out of me. We lived together but only had a platonic relationship, if that is what you can call it. The only thing we had in common was our children. I became bitter and started to dislike my wife, and even hate her at times. There were moments when I didn't even care if she was run over by a truck. How terrible that was! Here I was serving the Lord in the church, preaching from the pulpit at times, teaching people how to love one another, and yet I hated my wife. What a hypocrite! Many times I felt so guilty. I pleaded with God to change my heart and our situation. "You promised, Lord, that if we are faithful to You, You will take care of us." I remember our pastor saying to the congregation shortly after I became a Christian, "Come to Jesus, and all your problems will fly out the window." In my case, they all flew *in* the window when I became a Christian. I didn't have as many problems before I became a Christian. Now I was riddled with them.

Abrupt Turn of Events

One night, as I went to bed, I remember crying and telling God that I had had enough. "Please take my life instead of someone else who is meant to die because I can't handle this anymore. I am so drained, exhausted and empty. I don't have a speck of love left in me. I am riddled with bitterness, hatred and guilt. I cannot serve You any longer. Take me home to heaven."

At that moment, something incredible happened. It was as if I was on fire. The heat that entered my body was so intense that I thought I was going to blow up. Then it was as if someone had stuck a large funnel in my mouth and started pouring love into me. I mean, how do you explain this? My whole body and soul were enveloped, bathed in love. I realized then that it was the Lord Who was embracing me. I knew He loved and cared about me. I just cried and cried. I thought I was on my way to heaven since I had not experienced this intense feeling before. It was so beautiful and overwhelming. I didn't want it to stop. I wanted this to remain forever. Then the Lord spoke into my spirit and told me two things I had to do – pray for Berty's salvation and love her. I remember telling Him that I could pray for her, but I didn't have a speck of love left for her. That was all gone. It had been replaced with hate. Love was gone, and joy was gone. Happiness was also gone. If He wanted me to love her, He would have to give me His love for her and burn up my hate. The next thing I remembered, I woke up. It was definitely not a dream I had but I must have fallen asleep eventually.

When I awoke, I felt incredible. The first thing I noticed was that joy returned to me again. I jumped out of bed, whipped up a beautiful breakfast, and took it into my wife's bedroom. She was shocked beyond words. You could see on her face that she thought I had gone crazy. Then I got busy, cleaned the house and washed the dirty diapers. Joy overflowed as love became the driving force in my life. Our relationship didn't change. Really, things stayed the same or even got worse in a way, but it didn't affect me anymore like it had previously. I thanked God for her, and I thanked God for the day that was coming when she would give her life to the Lord. This went on for more than four years!

Then one evening a friend named Robert, who I hadn't seen for years, turned up for a visit. It was so good to see him again. We talked about all sorts of things - our families, our churches, and the good old days. The amazing thing was that my wife was in the lounge room with us. Normally she would be out with her friends in the pub or at their place, but this evening she stayed home and was reading a book while Robert and I were talking together. She had covered her face with the book so that we couldn't see her expression. However, she would frequently peer out from behind the book and ask a question pertaining to the spiritual subjects we were discussing late into the night. Finally, at three o'clock in the morning, Robert said, "Berty, from the questions you are asking me, I think what you really are saying is that you would like to receive Christ into your life." She replied, "Yes, I have been thinking about this for a while now, and I think the time has come." Robert prayed with her. The miracle of new birth happened.

What a change this made in our relationship. We started counseling sessions together, and through those sessions I learned so much about her that I didn't know. We were determined to make it work and we started to fall in love with each other all over again. It was just like being on our honeymoon. We went to church together - not always, but frequently - and peace filled our home. She would receive the most amazing dreams from the Lord sometimes and share them with me. She wondered what they meant. I can vividly remember one of those dreams. She said that as she was entering our church, suddenly the room was lit with bright golden rays of light with gold sprinkles floating everywhere. Love filled the place, and it was as if she were coming home. Then shortly after, she also told me about another dream. She said, "Three times now I have had the same dream that I died in a car accident. Do you think God is telling me something?" I told her not to be so ridiculous. What sort of a dream was that?

We were enjoying our lives together. Our children noticed the huge difference immediately. At the time, Berty and I were both working with intellectually disabled children and adults. Berty worked in a respite care house where families with an intellectually disabled child or adult could bring that child or adult to a home for a few days or weeks so that they could have a break. I worked in a home where six severely intellectually and physically disabled children and youth resided. We both enjoyed our jobs. This continued for about 18 months. Then tragedy struck. Tanja was 13, and our Paul was five.

My wife had decided to take one of her clients plus our two children for a ride one afternoon to a beautiful place in the hills called Beechworth. Something caused her to veer suddenly off the road. She struck a tree at high speed and totally destroyed the car. Both she and the client were killed, and our two children were severely injured with head injuries and fractures.

When I arrived home that day, there was a note on the table from my younger brother, who was boarding with us at the time. It said to call the hospital. When I called, a voice at the other end of the line told me to hurry to the hospital. "What's wrong? What has happened?" I asked. She said she could not provide me with any information. "Just get here as soon as you can," she urged, "and drive very carefully." I raced across the road to friends of ours from church and asked them to pray for Berty and the children. I feared something terrible had happened.

When I arrived at the hospital, the doctor met

me. “I’m very sorry,” he started. “Your wife is dead, and your children are severely injured. They are in the intensive care unit, and we don’t have much hope for them.” He requested that I join him in the morgue to identify Berty’s body.

As I walked down the hall to the morgue with my brother, I remembered my final words to my wife when leaving for work that morning: “Berty, I love you.” I was glad those were my last words to her. The doctor opened the door to a small, dimly lit room. It was cold and silent. On a stretcher in the middle of the room lay the mangled body of my wife. I just cried, shaking like a leaf. Time stood still for me. Yes, this was the body of my wife and friend, who, just a couple of hours before, joyously cruised down our driveway with her excited passengers. I confirmed the identification with the doctor and signed the necessary papers.

The doctor took my arm and led me down another hall to the intensive care unit. I choked with tears; my emotions were uncontrollable. There, lying on two beds, were my children. They had tubes coming from their bodies, and their heads were wrapped in large bandages. The life-support system was working hard. Blood was coming out of their ears, eyes, and nose. They were both in a deep coma and could not respond to my presence. The doctor motioned for my attention. I reluctantly approached him. “Mr. Heyboer, we really don’t think that your children will make it, but if they do pull through, they will definitely be vegetables," he said. "I'm very sorry." The children were in different rooms, and as I walked from one to the other holding their hands, I prayed. "God, I need You. Please heal my children."

Minutes slipped into hours, and the darkness of the night only added to my pain and anguish. After a few hours, the doctors determined that because the equipment at this smaller country hospital was limited, the children should be flown to the Royal Children's Hospital in Melbourne, an hour and a half away. On the flight I was trying to figure things out, but I was totally numb. How could this happen to us? "Oh, God, my God, why did You allow this to happen, just when things were so good?" I didn't understand. I wasn't mad at God. I just didn't understand. On the other hand, I was very grateful to the Lord that I had those 18 months with my wife, and that I knew where she was now. She was in the best place she could ever be.

At the Royal Children's Hospital, I was met by my cousin and her husband who had come to comfort me. The neurologist had arrived, and he also gave a pretty discouraging assessment. "We don't think they will make it through the night," he said, "but if they do, they will be vegetables and will have to remain here in this hospital for at least six months."

News spread quickly among church circles regarding what had happened to this youth leader and his family. People were coming from all over the place to see if they could do anything for me. They laid their hands on my children and prayed, "Child of God, be healed in the Mighty Name of Jesus." After four days I had to leave my children so I could attend Berty's funeral service. They were still in a coma, and lovely friends of ours stayed with them while I went home to attend the funeral. As I entered our home to get some more clothes for me to bring back to Melbourne, I remember smelling the fragrance of my wife throughout the house. I sobbed uncontrollably. I had to come to terms that I would never be able to hold her in my arms again. My mother and father had flown over to attend the funeral, as well as my wife's sister and her father. The service was recorded so that the children could hear the service on tape, if they survived.

The trip back to Melbourne was a sad one. Music from the last song at the funeral still floated in my mind. The sound of the dirt clods hitting the wooden box of my wife's coffin flooded my eyes with tears. After arriving in Melbourne, I hurried to the hospital to find that my children were beginning to show signs of waking from the coma, which was great news. Each day there was some slight improvement. Tanja's head injuries were more severe. When she came out of the coma, she screamed constantly and uttered words that didn't make sense at all. The doctors were worried that she might lose her eye as well. She had severe emotional wounds, and her mind was in turmoil for weeks. We would talk to her to find out what she could remember of the accident. Each day, she remembered a little more. She recalled getting up that morning and leaving home with the car, but she couldn't recollect anything about the accident or afterward. We had to repeat several times that Paul was also wounded and lying in another hospital room. We asked her if she knew what happened to Mum. She didn't know. After several days of asking her the same question in hopes that her memory would return, we revealed to her that Mum had died in the accident. Her expression did not change. She just responded, "Oh." However, the next day, she screamed a scream that could be heard throughout the building. A nurse hurried to get me because Tanja suddenly became hysterical. As I rushed in, she was standing on her bed shouting. When she spotted me, she yelled out over and over again, "You liar, you liar! Mum is not dead! She rang me last night and told me she was in another hospital!" She screamed things that no one could understand, like "Put some English on my side, quickly. Please put some English on my side." I had to leave the room quickly and burst into tears. Seeing my daughter in such a state, so muddled up as if she had lost her mind, was too much for me to handle. I thought then for a moment that perhaps God had prepared me for this since I had worked a number of years with intellectually disabled children. I could now look after my own children in such a state. Although I felt God's presence strongly with me during all that time, I was also confused about everything. Nothing seemed to make any sense.

Then the miracle happened! After just six weeks in the hospital, the children were released. The neurologist could not believe the dramatic healing that had taken place. "It's not possible," he insisted. "I've been a doctor for many decades, and I have seen things that I cannot explain. But what has happened with your children has topped the lot. It is impossible for anyone to be healed so rapidly after such injuries, and we are not talking about one person but two from the same family. We didn't do anything. You've definitely had help from somewhere else!"

After leaving the hospital in Melbourne, the children were transferred back to the local hospital in Wangaratta for a few weeks. Paul was still in plaster from his waist down with a fractured femur. Although Tanja still had her reservations about whether Mum was alive or dead, I felt she was more able now to handle the news of the accident. I showed her the front page newspaper article that reported the death of her mother. Tanja wept for hours, finally grasping the truth that Mum was indeed gone.

About eight weeks after the accident, the children were able to travel, so I took them to see the accident site. We found Mum's glasses under some tree bark. I took them to the wrecked car in the junkyard, to the ambulance drivers who cut them out of the car, then to the grave site. We held hands, we prayed, and we wept. I felt these painful experiences were necessary to help the children bring closure to the tragedy. Slowly, we made our way to the car and headed for home. It was time to start all over again.

The Call to Borneo

The children sobbed on the trip home from the cemetery. Their mother's death was now very real. Tanja and Paul loved their mum very much.

Once we got home, I had an important conversation with the children. Sitting them down in the front room of our house, I said something like this, "I cannot tell you why all this has happened, but God knows. We can go on for the rest of our lives asking why, but we will never get a satisfying answer. We can let resentment against God grow in our hearts, making us very bitter, but that will only destroy us. That would not please God. So let's pray, commit the matter to God, let Him fill our hearts with His joy, and get on with the things we were doing before the accident happened."

They agreed, and we all prayed. There was a peace filling our hearts and home. My ministry continued at the church, directing the activities of the youth and assisting in pastoral care for the congregation. The children went back to school and made their adjustments well.

Then something began to happen. The phone started ringing, and invitations to dinner came pouring in. I thought this was wonderful that so many ladies wanted to cook dinner for us! But after the fourth or fifth invitation, my delight turned into suspicion. These ladies were interested in *me* in the hope that I would be interested in them! That was very sweet of them, but I was not interested at all in anything at that moment. I turned down all further dinner invitations. Besides, I myself loved to cook, so we had good meals every night.

Living across the road from our house was a lovely Christian couple, Jill and Allen, with whom we frequently shared evenings of fellowship. On occasion, their family hosted a young nurse on the weekends. Her name was Kay. She had a happy, sparkling personality. I remember one day when I was going through sheer hell at home with Berty, I escaped to have a cup of coffee with Jill and Allen. Kay happened to be there, too. I thought then just for a split second how great it would be to have a wife like Kay who is so happy and bubbly. But I banished the thought because I was married. When Berty was still living, we would fellowship at Jill and Allen's house, and Kay was a frequent guest. Berty and I knew Kay from church; we also knew her parents and grandmother.

One day, my pastor pulled me aside, "Ronny, there's a wonderful youth conference on the Sunshine Coast (in the state of Queensland). Our church leaders believe it would do you good to attend and find some time to relax. We've arranged for the care of the children, and we will cover all of the expenses for the conference." I thought that it was a good idea, so I agreed. The arrangements were made: I was to board a bus heading to the conference. I learned that Kay would also travel to the event on the same bus. When the time came, I got on the bus, but there was only one vacant seat. It was right next to Kay. Maybe the church leaders had arranged this too, I thought.

The trip was long, so Kay and I talked for hours. At the conference, we agreed to eat together, sit together, and go shopping and swimming together in our free time. She was a great companion. We enjoyed the conference and our time together. During the four-day event, however, my thoughts ran wild because I started to feel something for Kay. But since I was still grieving for Berty, I did my best to suppress the feeling. On our bus ride home, we talked a lot. I couldn't stop wondering if God had put us together deliberately. Weeks before, I had a talk with God. I told Him, "God, I don't want to spend the rest of my life single. I need a wife and the children need a mother. If you would allow me to get married again, then I would like my future wife to have these qualifications. First, she must love You with all of her heart. She also must be beautiful within. Well, being beautiful in appearance also would be a bonus. She must accept and love my two children as her own. She must be willing to go anywhere in the world to serve You." As I talked to Kay on the bus, these qualifications were bubbling up in my mind. Beautiful? Yes. Love God? Yes. Love children? Yes. She was a nurse and worked with children. Open to going anywhere for Jesus? She indicated that very clearly as she shared her personal testimony of her Christian faith. But there was another qualification which was very important: She must not be in love with the things of this world. I wanted a wife whose values were spiritual, not material. So you can see that this whole trip and the long hours of conversation gave me an opportunity to assess Kay as a possible candidate for a wife. She seemed to qualify in every category. Besides meeting all these criteria, she was a happy, positive person. That impressed me. Frankly, the trip was too short for me. I wasn't sure how she was feeling about me, but I hoped that she felt the same way. I asked God to help me. "Lord, if You brought us together for a reason, then make it happen that we can talk and see each other regularly." Kay worked in Melbourne and I was in Wangaratta, almost a three-hour drive from each other. She said that she would come over and visit as soon as possible. That sounded promising.

Nothing of any serious nature transpired for the next three or four months. We would communicate through letters, frequent phone calls, and occasional visits when she was in town staying at our good friends' across the road. Some of my family and friends were very critical of the idea of me giving any attention to ladies. They felt that I should wait a year or two before dating. But I was the lonely bachelor, not them. A year and a month after Berty's death, Kay and I were married.

Tanja, then aged 15, rejected Kay at first. "You are not my mother, so quit telling me what to do!" she objected. Kay was patient and kind. She handled the situation with great wisdom. After a few years, Tanja changed her attitude. Soon, she and Kay became the best of friends.

As a result of the car accident, I received a substantial settlement from the insurance company. We paid off the mortgage on our beautiful home and settled all our debts. We had good savings and a very comfortable life. Both Kay and I had well-paying jobs, and married life could not be better. We were happy in our church ministries: Kay led the music ministry, while I helped the pastor care for the needs of our congregation. Still, there was a growing desire in our hearts to learn more about the Bible, and maybe, prepare for full-time ministry somewhere in the world.

In 1991, about a year after we married, I was planting seeds in my garden one afternoon when God began to speak to my spirit.

"Are you happy, Ronny?" He asked.

"Yes, I'm happy and grateful," I replied, "for all the blessings You have poured into my life!"

God then asked, "Are you satisfied, Ronny?"

Deep in my heart I wanted to be in the ministry. God knew that.

He said, "Pack up, sell up, and follow Me."

The message was so clear that I knew the call had come. I ran from the garden into the kitchen to share the thrilling news.

Kay's response, "Let's go. Call the real estate agent and put our house on the market. I'm ready."

You see, when Kay was 14 years old, she received a prophecy over her life that she would serve the Lord on the mission field. She knew this was the day for which God had prepared her, and she was ready.

After talking to the real estate agent, we called a Bible College in the northern part of Queensland to request enrollment information. We were so excited that we decided to visit the school. As it turned out, the school was a ministry of a very active mission-focused church, and that pleased us since we wanted to be missionaries. The campus also had a primary school and high school for our children. When we returned home, we told our pastor. He did not share our joy.

"That's definitely not of God," he concluded.

One of the church elders who happened to walk into the office heard our announcement.

"Pastor," he said, "I don't normally disagree with you, but this time I must. I believe God has called Ronny and Kay. I give them my blessing, and I want you to do the same."

For 15 minutes the pastor continued to press his point.

"You're busy here in our church," he said. "Your ministry is appreciated, and Kay is doing a wonderful job leading the music."

Finally, he realized he was not going anywhere with his argument, for I had already made up my mind. We were going to Bible College to prepare for a missionary ministry somewhere in the world! We didn't know where, but God did.

The conversation with the pastor ended with a prayer and his blessing. We resigned from our jobs.

Everyone else thought we were crazy because of the financial uncertainty everywhere. But we knew this was the right thing to do. God was going to look after us. We sold our house quickly at a substantial price. We loaded our furniture and other items in a truck, packed the car with the essentials, and started north on our journey. We were so happy, and God was with us. We knew, from the very beginning, that we were doing the right thing in our life.

In January 1992, we started Bible College. There were 24 students in the first class. We were all there because we felt God directing our lives; every mind and heart held great expectations for our unknown future. Kay was a part-time student. She also worked some hours each week to provide income for our family. Classes were very difficult for me. Remember, I was kicked out of school when I was 16, and books and tests were not a part of my life. I had to study many more hours a day than the younger students who had just finished university. But I made it with good grades. Kay was very helpful. I wrote my assignments, she would correct the spelling, then I could rewrite them for my final presentations. At the start of the second year, I was voted Head Student. Of course, my love for missions created the theme for all our activities at the college. We developed many projects, bringing in funds for missions. The college was only a two-year program so we graduated in December 1993 with a distinction of honor.

Having finished our schooling, we pondered

the next stage of our journey. What did God want us to do? Where did He want us to spend our life in Christian work? We knew it had to be on the mission field, but we needed Him to show us precisely where. I felt the need to do a 40-day fast. I had never done such a long fast before, usually just a few days or a week. This time the urge to desperately seek God's will through a long fast seemed the right thing to do. I found that I was much more sensitive to the voice of the Lord during times of prayer and fasting.

I had developed a friendship with someone at Bible College who had a burden to plant churches on the island of Flores (Indonesia). He wanted to go with his wife and children to do some reconnaissance work first before moving there. I didn't think it was a good idea to take his family on that first trip, but I volunteered to accompany him for support. Our missions committee thought it was a good idea. Two weeks before we left we had an all-night prayer meeting at the Bible College, and around three in the morning, the Lord revealed to us that we should also go to Borneo. My friend and I were puzzled. Why go to Borneo? It is thousands of kilometers away from Flores. We thought perhaps God was showing my friend a way to get the right visas for serving in Flores. Again the missions committee agreed to the plan. And in the end, it turned out being cheaper to go to Borneo before heading to Flores.

We landed at the seaport city of Pontianak, located in West Kalimantan, in the Indonesian part of Borneo. Stepping off the plane my heart started to race. I had the same feeling when I arrived in Melbourne after being in Holland for ten years. It felt like coming home. But I remember telling the Lord that I wasn't here for me but for my friend. However, the Holy Spirit kept on witnessing in my heart that it was here where God wanted us to serve in the work of His kingdom. Local ministers met us and invited us to speak at local churches and visit some of the tribes on the river. My assignment was to ride a boat up the river to a large sawmill. Scattered throughout the jungle were people who worked at the mill. And when it came time for the evening meeting, hundreds and hundreds of people poured into a large building. In all, 4,000 people worked at the sawmill, and they were coming to hear me speak! I was completely surprised. What was I going to say? I had never preached to a crowd this huge. However, days before coming to Borneo, I had read a book on the Father-heart of God, and many ideas from that book flooded my mind. I quickly organized my thoughts. Finally, I was ready. The response simply amazed me. When I gave the call to receive Christ, hundreds came forward for prayer. As our little boat made its way back to Pontianak, my heart was so much at peace. I knew where God wanted us to work in His vineyard – here in the jungles of Borneo. I just needed to let Kay know.

As soon as we arrived back in Australia, I told Kay that I knew where God wanted us to be – in Borneo. She said, "Well let's get going then." But I wanted to make sure that this was God's will and not merely my will. I went to see the Bible College principal and asked him how I would know what God's will was.

His answer to me was simple. He said, "Ronny, do you love God?"

"Yes," I replied, "you know I do."

"Do you desire to do God's will?" was his next question.

"Yes, of course I desire to do God's will, more than anything else in this world."

"Then if you think that going to Borneo is God's will, but it actually isn't, do you think God would let you go?"

"No," I replied. "He wouldn't. He would stop me."

"Exactly. God is your Father, and He would stop you. As for me," he said, "I believe God has opened a door for you in Borneo and you should go. But like I said, if it isn't His doing, then He will shut the door on you."

When I arrived home I read the portion in the book of Acts, Chapter 16, where Paul was on his way to Ephesus to plant a church. However, half way there, the Holy Spirit stopped him but said nothing. Paul didn't sit around or go back to Antioch, but instead, he thought it a good idea to go to Bithynia to share the Gospel. But again the Holy Spirit stopped him in his tracks. Again no communication happened, so Paul then decided to go on to Troas. It was there that he received the vision of a man pleading with him to go to Macedonia. Paul responded immediately and headed for Philippi. As a result, Europe became Paul's vision and challenge. So here was a missionary who desired also, more than anything else, to do God's will, though His will wasn't always clear to him. He thought that God wanted him to go to Ephesus, yet God had other plans. If Paul didn't always know, then I think I am not always going to know either. I have learned over the years that when God puts something on my heart, then I always say to Him, "God, I believe You want me to do this, but if I didn't get this right, then please forgive me, stop me, and steer me in the right direction. I want to go to the place You want me to be." I felt the call to Borneo was God's will for Kay and me. In fact, when I met with some of the church board members, they said that even before my friend and I went to Borneo, God had already revealed to them that Kay and I would end up there. I was amazed and asked why they didn't tell us earlier. They responded, "We wanted the Lord to reveal and confirm this to you."

Our daughter Tanja had just turned 19, and she had no desire to come with us. She was looking forward to some independence, but she encouraged us to obey God and proceed to Borneo. She reassured us that she would be fine; we need not worry about her because she could look after herself pretty well.

And so with our sons, Paul, age 11, and Nathaniel, almost two, we packed some of our household goods and suitcases. We flew to Kuching, in the western section of Borneo, known as Sarawak, a province governed by Malaysia. Sarawak is much more developed than Kalimantan, the Indonesian province just across the border. We were filled with great hopes and dreams as we started our first year working with a local missionary. Unfortunately we realized that missionaries were just as human as other people, and some of them were downright dishonest and unfair. Our first year was extremely difficult because we learned there was wrongdoing going on that needed to be exposed and changed. We just could not work under the existing conditions. After much prayer and wisdom sought from more experienced missionaries, we learned that many of them were equally aware of the problem. They felt they could do nothing about it, so they just kept silent. Kay and I refused to be a part of the cover-up. On the advice of our pastor in Australia, I decided to confront the guilty person. He responded angrily and retaliated. He called my pastor in Australia and demanded that we be recalled immediately. He reported that we were unqualified to fit into the culture. He arranged for all of our missionary activities to be stopped at once. Instead, we were to be reviewed by a missionary committee whose members he himself selected. He also sent a letter to the board members of our church in Australia, who responded by sending us a letter demanding our return home. I went back, and the board was ready to believe the accusations. But thank God for wise pastors! After consulting other missionaries about the problem, our pastor directed me to return to Borneo with the church's blessing and support. Within months, the man who had made life unbearable for us was beginning to lose his influence, as other missionaries confirmed he was abusing mission funds. Thank God, our church pastor in Australia wisely handled the matter, and our ministry continued on the island of Borneo.

The personal attack wasn't our only major challenge. There was also an epidemic raging in Borneo. A mysterious virus was infecting the membrane around the heart of children aged five years and under. Hundreds, if not thousands, of children filled hospitals all over the island. Many died. The Malaysian government brought in their experts and other scientists from the United States to find out what this mysterious virus was, and how it was transmitted, whether through the air, water, or food, etc. All schools and public places were closed until it was safe again. Finally they discovered the culprit was a hand-foot-and-mouth disease with a Coxsackie B strain. Expatriates and many wealthy Chinese left the island for Singapore or Hong Kong until the epidemic was over. We were warned to leave Borneo as well because Nathaniel was only two years old, but we felt that we had to remain and face the situation, trusting God to help us through. The epidemic passed after a few months.

The first year ended with a great spiritual victory. The epidemic had passed, our accuser was silenced, and the restrictions on our missionary activity had been lifted. We decided earlier that we would affiliate our mission with World Outreach. Hundreds of other missionaries from around the world also joined the interdenominational mission organization. World Outreach was not an agency which would raise funds and sponsorship for missionaries, but it had strong fellowship and support in areas like pastoral care, accountability, training, and teaching.

During this first year, Kay and I became acquainted with a missionary couple who had a similar burden to work among the Dayak tribal people, planting churches and caring for orphaned children, or any children in crisis. They had already been living in Sanggau for three years before we arrived. The town was deeper in the interior. We decided together with World Outreach that this was a good place for us to partner in ministry.

Our partnership there was exciting and challenging. Working with this couple was beneficial to both sides, as we each possessed talents that blended and strengthened the other's ministry. Together we gave our ministry a name, New Hope Ministries, and outlined its structure. The other missionary assumed the main responsibility of directing the affairs of the ministry, while I went from village to village, preaching, planting churches, and pastoring church planters. We were an effective and productive team.

The first children we helped as part of New Hope Ministries were seven girls. We found that many young girls aged 11 to 14, who began to menstruate, would often be given in marriage to some old tribal guy who already had a few wives, but wanted to acquire another virgin. In exchange, her family would usually receive a few pigs, some cash or both. This allowed her relatives to breed the pigs and have a little business so they could survive. Often the girl would become pregnant straight away, and by the time she was 20 years old, she already would have given birth to four to five children. By the time she was 25 years old, she looked like an old woman. As I witnessed such a wedding one day, I couldn't help but grieve for the girl. She was crying, knowing full well what her future held. It even crossed my mind before the ceremony took place to grab her and run for our lives, but that would be rather foolish as they would certainly come after us, and no doubt the consequences would be serious for me. Hence, it was a priority to rescue girls. We rented a house for them and had one of our leaders stay there as a house parent. Although this was a good idea, we really did not have the money to look after them. We had no money for their food, clothes and school fees, but God assured us that He would provide. At the end of the month when the bills had to be paid, enough extra money had arrived from sponsors to pay all the bills. Not too much and not too little, but just enough. Needless to say our faith was strengthened. We were so excited. So we said to the Lord, "If You can do it for seven girls, then You can also do it for 30 girls." And so a few months later, our house was filled with 30 girls, and the same thing happened. Just enough money had arrived from various sponsors. Not too much and not too little, but just enough to pay all the bills. Again, we were so excited! Our faith was being stretched more and more, and we were being challenged. We learned to believe that our God can do anything if we just believe and obey. So again we said to God, "If You can do it for 30 girls, then You can also do it for 70 children." But this time we had to look for land, since the landlord was not happy with 30 girls living in the house. Again, we had no money, but that was not going to stop us. We prayed for the right piece of land in Sanggau so that we could house not only the girls, but also boys in desperate need of help. A few weeks later, enough money had arrived from an anonymous donor to buy a piece of land that was most suitable for our ministry there. What an incredible blessing! God was teaching us and testing our faith to see if we truly believed that nothing is impossible with Him.

But the enemy was obviously not happy with our plans, and tried several times to get rid of us. When we believe in God, yet do not step out in faith and do not really believe that God can make possible the impossible, we are disobedient. Our faith has no power, and we are then not a threat to the enemy. Faith has to be activated through belief and obedience. If we know who we are in Christ, and know we have been given authority and power over the enemy, there is nothing impossible for God. If we use our God-given talents and gifts to step out in faith and accomplish the work He has set before us, then our faith is active, and God will do His miracles through His Holy Spirit living in us. It is then that we are a threat to the enemy, a big threat, and he is not going to like that. He will try to do whatever he can to stop us abruptly or gradually. If he cannot do it quickly or forcibly, then he will try to do it in a cunning, sneaky way. He will target our weaknesses, so we need to be on guard all the time. However, if we know who we are in Christ, then we will not be afraid.

Shortly after our arrival in Sanggau, I got sick. I was so sick that doctors thought I had contracted malaria or typhoid. Day after day the sickness grew worse. I could not tolerate any light at all. The pain in my head and eyes felt excruciating. My stomach was in turmoil and my fever would come and go throughout the day and night. One of the doctors at the local hospital started to treat me for malaria, but my sickness became even more acute.

After a week, Kay insisted on driving me to Kuching. I was so weak I couldn't even get out of the car at the border. Kay drove straight to Timberland Hospital. As soon as the doctor had examined me, he also believed it was typhoid or malaria. But a blood test proved it was neither. My stomach, head and eyes were in tremendous pain. I felt nauseous all the time. I thought I was dying. With my body hooked to all kinds of tubes, I continued to deteriorate. The doctor suggested that I could be suffering from leptospirosis, which results from bathing in water where rats and pigs had urinated. A year before, many people in Thailand died of the disease. It affects the liver and the kidneys, and my liver and kidneys were beginning to show signs of damage. The doctor asked Kay if I had been exposed to water where pigs and rats urinated. He was surprised when she told him that on my travels into the jungle, I frequently bathed in contaminated water where the tribal people also bathed. The doctor explained that the disease could enter through a wound or the eyes, infecting the bloodstream. The doctor took more blood tests, which had to be sent to Adelaide, Australia, because they didn't have the proper testing facilities in Malaysia. Then on a Sunday afternoon, I suddenly started to improve. It was a wonderful feeling. The doctor did his patient rounds. When he came to my bedside, he was astonished. "Wow!" he exclaimed. "You're looking so much better. Well, one of the medicines must be working. I don't know which one, but that doesn't really matter. You're improving!" I was recovering so rapidly that he discharged me from the hospital on Tuesday. I was still very weak but well enough to go home.

As I recuperated, I began looking over my emails. A message had arrived from a little church in Mareeba in North Queensland, Australia. In essence, this was what it said, "Brother Ronny, we didn't know you were so sick, but here's what happened last Sunday during our morning service. Our pastor was preaching but stopped half way through the message and said that the Holy Spirit was revealing that we had to pray for one of our missionaries who was very sick. In fact, it was a matter of life and death, and we all had to pray and intercede for his life. We prayed and interceded and begged the Lord to heal the person even though the Holy Spirit didn't reveal who it was. After a while, some people felt that there was a breakthrough; we thanked the Lord, and the pastor continued with the sermon. The next day, World Outreach Australia called our church to say that Ronny Heyboer was seriously ill in the hospital. Then we realized we prayed for you." As I was reading this email, I started to get goose bumps and teary eyes. I was reminded of what the doctor said on Sunday afternoon, "Wow! You're looking so much better. One of the medicines must be working. I don't know which one, but that doesn't really matter." So it wasn't the medicine after all, but a small group of people somewhere in North Queensland who were told to pray and obeyed the Lord. As a result, I was healed. Wow! What a miracle! Now why does God operate like that? Isn't He God? Couldn't He have just healed me Himself without having to call someone to pray for me? Of course, He could have. After all, He created the universe and mankind. If He could do that, then He could certainly heal me. But He often chooses to perform His miracles through the body of Christ.

One day, when I was visiting a remote village, I came across a man who had accidentally cut off his thumb with a chainsaw. His thumb quickly shriveled up and died, because it wasn't connected to the oxygen, blood flow, and warmth from the body that it needed to stay alive. It's the same when missionaries are sent out. They must remain connected with their church, the body of Christ, receiving love, care, prayer, and fellowship. God doesn't want us to just send them off and say, "I'm glad that it's you going, brother, and not me. We will try to remember you and send something now and then." I believe the Lord wants us to care for our missionaries well. Pray for them regularly for protection and provision for their needs. Pray also that they will remain connected to the family of God back home. Six months after this miracle happened, I visited that small church in North Queensland, Australia, and thanked them for being so faithful and obedient. Their obedience made it possible for me to stand before them, healed, and able to testify about the greatness of our God, and how much He desires His people to believe that anything is possible with Him.

Challenges in Sanggau

Our youngest child, Joel, was born in Australia while we were on our first furlough. When we arrived back at home in Borneo's jungle, he was only a few months old. We decided as a family to visit some of our churches in the interior to encourage our young pastors and their congregations. When we arrived at one of the villages belonging to the Matee tribe, we received a warm welcome. However, Kay and Joel were excluded from the greeting. In fact, the women and children in particular kept quite a distance from them, looking worried and even frightened. This behavior was rather peculiar, since the tribal people are usually very hospitable. When I asked our church planter about it, he asked them directly. He discovered that the women and children had never seen a white baby before. In fact, they were amazed to know that "White Man" had babies too. They presumed that White Man were as it says white "man" only. And because Joel was also bald, they concluded he must be an evil spirit. Their babies are always born with lots of black hair. For them to see a baby who was bald and as white as milk was unheard of. Anything out of the ordinary in their culture is often immediately assumed to be part of the spirit world. When we assured them that White Man definitely have babies too and that Joel was definitely not an evil spirit but an ordinary child of White Man, they started to relax. Some took courage and came closer to greet Kay and Joel. However, not everyone was convinced. They needed a bit more time to come to terms with this new revelation. Years later, when some of our little girls in the children's home received a Christmas gift of a bald white baby doll, they started to cry hysterically. They didn't want anything to do with it. We realized that their fear of bald white babies had been passed on even though they had seen a number of white babies at our place. It was already ingrained in their belief system. What a mystery really.

Shortly after my sickness and miraculous recovery, the enemy made another attempt to destroy me. I was driving to the border to pick up a team of people from the *Doulos* ship who were coming to help us at the children´s home. I was on my own and driving at a safe speed, approximately 20 minutes from the border. While entering a small village, I looked to my right and then to my left. I saw this little old lady standing on the edge of the road wanting to cross over. We had eye contact so I knew she saw me coming, and thus, she should have waited before crossing the road. Suddenly, she lunged out in front of my car. I tried swerving to avoid her. But after a loud thud, she flew into the air, and landed in the grass on the side of the road. I screamed out to Jesus. I stopped my car, jumped out, and ran over to her. Blood was flowing from her ears, nose and mouth. I knew she was badly injured. Two men came running up to the car. I knew that at any moment they could slit my throat because the old tribal law is a life for a life, regardless of whose fault it was. I'd been warned when I first came to this island, never to stop if I hit someone, but continue to the nearest police station and report the accident. I couldn't do that. My conscience wouldn't allow it. I had to stop and see if I could do something for her. Thankfully, the men didn't come after me. Instead, they tried to calm me down. I was shaking and crying. I asked them to help me to take her to the hospital since she was still breathing. However, when the men saw the woman, they said, "Oh, it is her. Don't worry. She jumps in front of cars. She does this all the time. Normally, she is locked up in that house over there, but she obviously escaped. Well, she has made a real mess this time. We will take care of her. You just go to the police station and report the matter." By this time, more people had arrived. I asked if two people could accompany me to the police station for support. As I got back into the car, I saw the first two men grab the woman by her arms and legs and move her farther from the road. They were rough with her. They treated her as if she were just an animal. It was very disturbing. Apparently, half an hour later she died. I believe that she was left there to die, without any medical attention. She was worth more dead than alive. If she lived they would have received nothing, but in her death, the tribe would receive compensation. In addition, she wouldn't be a burden in the village any longer.

I reported the incident to local police nearby. They quickly transferred me to police headquarters in Sanggau. They feared a riot, which often happens at road accidents, especially when someone is killed. I was eventually charged, and then to my horror, jailed. The officer abruptly told me that I would be there for the next five years!

"But I didn't do anything wrong!" I explained. "She was the one who jumped in front of my car."

"But she's dead, sir," he answered, "and you're alive. So you must stay in jail for five years. You'll go to court. The judges will determine if you will stay in jail, pay compensation, or both. Most likely you will get five years."

I couldn't believe this turn of events. Many thoughts were spinning in my mind. "How can this be possible? What can I do? What is Kay going to do? How about our children and all the other children in our care? God, this isn't happening. I don't want to be here. I don't want to start a prison ministry. That wasn't part of the plan, right, God? Please help and rescue me, Lord." I spent the first three days in jail crying and feeling sorry for myself. The place was rat-infested and the fleas were too numerous to count. Kay was allowed to bring me some food each day. I apparently had some privileges that others didn't, perhaps because I was a foreigner. The police did report the incident to the Australian Embassy, but we never received any response from them. Kay was also allowed to bring my Bible, a thin rolled-up mattress, and clean clothes. There were no toilets in the cells. I asked the jailer what to do when I needed to use the bathroom. In the corner of the cell was an empty plastic bottle. He told me to use it when I needed to go. Then he said, "When you're finished, just dump it out the window."

"But what about number two?" I asked.

"Well," he said, "when you need to do number two, just let us know, and we'll take you out to a toilet."

I couldn't believe it. The first time I called them, two police officers arrived with machine guns. They escorted me, sandwiched between them as if I were some sort of murderer. They remained there while I relieved myself. Did they think I would escape with my pants down? I could just see it. That would have been a sight.

The cell wreaked of mildew, tobacco smoke, and urine. It was truly unbearable at times. After three days, I decided to stop whining. I told God, "Okay, if I am here for five years, well, then I am here for five years. I can't do anything about it. I'd better make the most of it." I didn't understand why this was happening, but that wasn't anything new. A lot of things that happened in my life I didn't understand. I had already learned that I didn't have to understand everything, anyway. As long as God knew what He was doing, it must be okay. I knew that He loved me, and if I was doing His will, then nothing would happen to me without His permission. *He* decides what happens to me, not the enemy. That doesn't mean that nothing bad ever happens to us. It doesn't say anywhere in the Bible that we will not have any problems or nasty painful situations in our lifetime. But it does tell us that He is always with us, and will carry us through our darkest moments because He cares for us and will never leave us. Besides, many of the dark moments in my life have actually helped me to grow in my faith and dependence on God. Our faith needs to be tested, molded, and shaped. That cannot be accomplished if we never go through difficult times.

Kay and the children were allowed to visit. It was a wonderful privilege. Each visit provided me with some food and clean clothing, but there was one thing that left the jailer speechless: all our other children! At the time of this event, we had about 200 children in our children's home. Of course, they all wanted to visit Bapak. Each time, 10 to 20 children turned up at the police station to see me. I remember when the first group arrived. Apparently they told the police officer on duty that they wanted to see their father.

The police officer said "And who might that be?"

The children declared, "Bapak Ronny."

"Pak Ronny the White Man is your father?"

"Yes, he is our father, and you have no right to lock him up. We demand you release him now."

I was escorted again in between two police officers with machine guns into the visiting area where the children waited. When they spotted me unshaven and disheveled, they began to cry so loud that just about everyone came out of their offices to see the reason for the commotion. We hugged each other and prayed together in full view of all the police officers. After 20 minutes, they were told to go home. We said goodbye, and I was escorted back to my cell. But that didn't last very long because half an hour later, the next 10 to 20 children arrived to see Bapak Ronny. This went on for quite some time until it became the talk of the town.

I was so comforted that I was allowed to have my Bible. One of my cell mates, who was imprisoned for theft, kept watching me read and pray. Eventually he asked, "Who is this God of yours? It is like you are married to Him the way you talk to Him." He started to ask many questions. Anton was his name. One day, a police officer marched into our cell and started beating and kicking Anton furiously. I became angry, and yet I was afraid, not knowing if I should intervene. The police officer eventually addressed me with fiery eyes, "This kid is from my tribe and has brought great shame to me and my people by stealing motorbikes. If he were in the village right now, his punishment would be far worse." I realized that this was their way of dealing with such problems. Tribal law is very different but often very effective for its people.

While in prison, I had plenty of time on my hands. I asked Kay to bring me the envelopes for our next newsletter so that I could write a personal note to each person on our address list. At that time, I think we had about 400 people in our database. I wrote each one saying that I felt just like the Apostle Paul when he was in prison, except that my back was not ripped open like his, and my hands and feet were not chained. I knew that God was with me, and that He had everything under control even though I didn't know His plan yet. I asked people to pray and encouraged them by saying they should never give up hope, whatever their situation. I finished each note thanking them for their marvelous support of God's work here in Borneo. Soon I received replies to my letters. A number of people wrote to say that God had used my words to rebuke them because they were complaining to God at the time about very unimportant things. They said it was as if the Lord hit them between the eyes with a piece of wood. Some said they started to cry and asked forgiveness. Of course they were not alone. At times all of us whine and complain about all sorts of things that are not even important. But you know, each time we do that, we are really saying to God that we are not satisfied with the way He blesses us each day. We all should be more grateful for the way God takes care of us. We take so much for granted every day. We should stop more often and think about all the things we have, not the things we don't have, and thank the Lord sincerely for all His blessings.

Hundreds of kilometers away in Pontianak, a Christian men's conference was underway. The men got word of my imprisonment and they began to pray. At the conference was a friend who was the retired police chief of that province. As soon as he heard I was jailed, he rounded up a group of four or five pastors to visit me. It was a long trip, and his sudden, unannounced arrival without official escorts alarmed the local authorities. Although he was retired, he still retained high respect and honor wherever he went. So his sudden arrival at the police station alarmed everyone there. As he walked in, his first words were, “Where is my friend Pak Ronny?” The police officers on duty looked at each other and realized this was going to be interesting. They hastily escorted me from my cell to the visitors’ room where we embraced each other. He said, “I will go and speak with the chief of police to get you out of here. Don’t worry, all will be okay.” A short time later, he returned and said that I would be released on Monday, but I would still be under town arrest until the court case came up. We prayed together, and he went back to Pontianak. I was completely stunned at the turn of events. I never knew that this retired friend was a former police chief. I only knew him as a brother in the faith.

Monday arrived, and I was released from prison. What a wonderful feeling! What a glorious gift from God to be free! I was placed under town arrest until the court hearing took place a couple of months later. We had already settled the matter with the tribe: we paid approximately $2,000 in American currency, compensation which was to be shared with the family of the deceased, but also some of the elders of the tribe.

Because I was under town arrest, I couldn’t leave town and visit our villages where a number of our church planters were located. Instead, I knocked on the door of the jail and asked if I could see some of the prisoners. The jailors were glad to see me. It had occurred to me that God had opened a door for me to go into the prison with my Bible. This would never have been possible prior to the accident. They didn't know me then and would have certainly told me to go away. But now they knew me and welcomed me in. I visited my friend Anton. Shortly after, he gave his life to Jesus. Because of his marked change of attitude and behavior, the authorities reduced his sentence and released him from prison. He came to stay with us, and God used him instrumentally in the new vision God placed on our hearts. Years later, he returned to his tribe, a notoriously hostile tribe, to look after his mother and to bring the Gospel to them. How awesome is that? Who would have thought that such good would come out of such a mess? God knew, of course. He allows these situations all the time. He loves mankind, those who are saved and those who are lost. And at times, He will even call some of His loved ones to suffer for a while, or even sacrifice them, in order to rescue the lost. You see, those who are already saved know that when they die they will go to heaven and live with our Lord forever, but not so with those who don't have a relationship with Christ. God wants to give every person on this planet the opportunity in this life to come to know Him, and He will even use some of His own children who are already saved to try to accomplish this. Try? Yes, try, because man still has to make the choice to decide whether to receive Him or reject Him. He will not make that choice for us. What a wonderful Heavenly Father we have!

When my court date arrived, the room was full. We faced three judges. Then there was the district attorney. He hated me simply because I was a foreigner and a Christian. He was not a local from Borneo but from another island, Sumatra. I was represented by a lady who would be the equivalent of a paralegal. She could speak some English.

The wrangling went on for hours between the judges and the district attorney. Finally, the tribal chief from the area where the accident occurred stood to speak. He was told to sit down, but he refused. "I will not sit down. I have something to say. Why is this man still here? This man has paid our tribe compensation for the woman. He's done everything according to our tribal law. Is he here because you're trying to extort money from him?"

"Sit down," demanded the district attorney.

"I will not sit down until you release this man," the tribal chief insisted.

Soon my release was granted. I was ordered to pay a fine amounting to 2,000 Rupiah. How much was that? Twenty cents! Eight days in jail, a USD2,000 tribal fee, a 20-cent fine, and I was free.

Back home that evening, I rejoiced together with my children, my wife, and all of our other children and fellow missionaries. We thanked God for His marvelous miracle!

After my release, some of our young men met the district attorney at the local post office where his wife worked. In a sarcastic tone, he pronounced the sentence a farce. "He should have received five years," he said. "Who does he think he is anyway, and what is he to you?"

My boys retorted, "He is like a father to us, someone who actually cares for us, not like others. If anything should happen to him, we know where to find you."

They said the man turned pale with fear for he knew all too well what the locals in Borneo were capable of doing. Someone once said to me, "Oh, you work among the former headhunters." I replied, "Yes, but some are still headhunters." The district attorney knew that very well. I am not implying that my boys would resort to violence, God forbid. They intended to scare the man, and they obviously succeeded.

Months later, as I was on my way to the border with two of our young men to pick up another team of visitors, we were stopped at a road block where many police officers and military personnel were searching all passing vehicles. From a distance, it looked like quite an operation. As the police officers walked up to my car, a commander flung open my door and ordered, "Get out of the car! We're going to search it!" Usually, police are quite respectful, but this was the first time I had encountered an officer who was so upset. Maybe he was looking for something important like drugs or weapons. As I was getting out of the car, I noticed another police officer dashing out of a building behind me. He approached the commander. I could hear him say, "This is that pastor with all those kids who was locked up awhile ago for that accident." Immediately, the commander's expression softened. He said, "Oh yes, oh my goodness. Sorry, sorry. I have heard all about you. Please get back into your car. Everything is okay." Then he ordered the officers to back off from my car. He instructed others to let me through. I was completely baffled at the turn of events. I realized that my time in jail actually did a lot of good, because many high-ranking officials had heard about this long-nosed white missionary. Apparently it was the talk of the town then. I had no idea, but God knew.

The Terrible Onslaught

While I was on a ministry trip in Holland, a Christian brother informed me of what he had just read in the newspaper. The border between Malaysia and Indonesia on the island of Borneo had been closed. A tribal war had broken out between the Dayaks, the natives of Borneo, and the Madurese, people from Madura Island, which is located just above the island of Java. They had migrated to Borneo through the transmigration scheme set up by the government.

I quickly telephoned Kay to find out if this was true. Indeed, the border was closed. According to reports, all hell had broken loose within Kalimantan. People who used to be the best of friends were now killing each other. The whole thing started in the

Sambas region when apparently a bus driver refused to give a passenger a ticket. Both were from different tribal groups. When one of them was killed, revenge spread across the area like wild fire. People were murdering each other without really knowing why. The Madurese were killing the Dayaks or anyone who looked like a Dayak. When they weren't sure, they would smell the person because each people group had a particular smell about them from their diet. The Dayaks were lopping off the heads of Madurese and placing them on sticks and poles as trophies to show off to everyone. Poles with heads were displayed everywhere, but usually at the side of the road before entering a village or town. Pontianak had poles with heads displayed in front of the main bridge at the city entrance as a warning. The Dayaks were well known for their head hunting past, but unfortunately it was still practiced in remote regions of the island even though the government declared it illegal. Officials and medical staff estimated that about 6,000 people were butchered to death, mostly by decapitation. Part of the ritual is not only to kill the enemy but also to eat some of their flesh and drink some of their blood. They call this "sakti." They believe that they then become supernaturally stronger than their enemy. It is a demonic ritual that puts a curse on their lives. It demonstrates that without Christ life is cheap and has little value. How these people desperately need Jesus to set them free from these demonic practices!

Most of the dead were Madurese, as the

Dayaks had the upper hand. After all, this was their territory, and they were defending it at any cost. An estimated 20,000 Madurese women and children took refuge in Pontianak, the capital. They were housed in the grand stadium of the city. They lived there for a number of years in horrendous conditions. They feared for their lives. Their husbands, fathers and brothers had all been killed. They had nothing left. Their homes burned down. They were too afraid to return. The city officials didn't know what to do with them. Years later, the government decided to send them back to Madura.

Kay assured me she was safe from the violence, but I quickly packed up in Holland and headed home. I was worried for our church planters and new churches filled with young Christians. I hoped that none of them were forced to participate in this revenge killing and slip back into the demonic ritual.

As I arrived in Kuching, I was told that the borders reopened. That was good news. The next day I took my son, Paul, who was then 13, and headed for the border. As we entered the Indonesian side, a police officer said to me, "Where do you think you are going?"

"We are going to Sanggau," I replied.

"No, do not go there. It is still unsafe."

Paul was worried. "Dad, he says we shouldn't go in. We need to go back to Kuching."

To put Paul's mind at ease, I asked the police

officer, "It is now eleven o'clock in the morning, so how many cars have already gone through?"

"None," he said. "You are the first one."

I was surprised to hear that, but in my continuing effort to reassure Paul, I asked, "Yesterday the border reopened, right? So how many cars went through then?"

He said, "One, and he never returned."

"See, Dad?" Paul remained worried.

Then I pointed to our car and asked Paul, "Can't you see all of God's angels around our car?"

He looked puzzled, yet stared intently at our car. "No, I can't see them. Can you?"

"No, I can't see them either," I answered, "but I know they are there. The Word of God says so. We have to go, and God will be with us. We have His assurance."

So we left the border and made our way into the "unsafe zone" as it was called. As we were driving along, we were shocked to see the massive destruction. Some villages had burned to the ground. It smelled terrible everywhere. Apparently many bodies were still not buried days after they were killed. In humid, tropical weather, bodies decompose rapidly, so they are usually buried the next day. The government had to bring in a special regiment of the army from Jakarta to help dispose of all the bodies. Weeks later, we heard of many atrocities that had occurred in various places. At the bus junction in Sosok, more than 300 men and boys were butchered to death. It was a horrendous blood bath that scarred many people in the region emotionally for many years, even up until today.

We made our way to Sanggau. When we arrived at the rented house, the house leader and others were astounded to see us. "What are you doing here, Pak Ronny?" he asked. "You cannot possibly stay here because if they (the enemy) know that you are here, they will come after you. They are randomly going around at night and killing people. You must go back before it is too late." I was shocked, not at his response, but at the way he and the others looked. Their eyes were blood shot from having not slept in 48 hours. An intense fear covered their faces. They looked like death warmed up. I noticed nothing but fear in their eyes and voices so I quickly urged them to sit down. I read to them scripture after scripture of God's greatness, presence and peace. I prayed that God's peace would envelop them. Then I told them to go to sleep. "All will be well. Trust in the Lord your God." Some slept for an incredible 22 hours! Their bodies were totally exhausted.

Days later, when it was somewhat safer to travel, we went to all our churches in the interior to meet up with them and find out how this whole tribal war had affected them. We were so happy to see and hear how all of them refused to participate in the revenge killing. One of our church planters told us that at one point, some tribal leaders distributed enemy body parts to the various villages for people to participate in the "sakti" ritual. But the new converts did not want anything to do with it anymore because now they were Christians with their trust and hope in Jesus. Praise God! What wonderful news this was!

We kept on thanking the Lord for His love and protection. Since then God has blessed these new Christians abundantly with a peace and love for each other. Many new families came into the Kingdom of God as a result. It was so amazing to see how husbands were now treating their wives, no longer as slaves, but as friends. Fathers were now helping to look after their children and assisting with the heavy manual labour, duties that were previously the responsibility of women. God has so blessed them. All glory to Him.

Years later, I was talking around our kitchen table to some of our young people about the unconditional love of Jesus. I told them that Jesus loves all mankind, all tribes, and all people groups. One of our boys stopped me abruptly. "No," he stated, "that is not possible. Jesus could not possibly love the Madurese. They are worse than dogs. They have slaughtered my people."

I explained, "Oh yes, He does love them very much. He died for them as well so that they, too, can have their sins forgiven and be set free from bondage."

He looked shocked and puzzled as he listened to me. A few moments later I noticed a few tears rolling down his face. I asked him what was wrong. He stared at me at first for a little while, his big brown eyes filling up with tears. I could tell it was going to be difficult for him to share. He said, "While the onslaught was happening all around us, I shot two children through the head and killed them. They were Madurese and not worth living."

I was stunned. "How could you have done that?" I asked.

He said, "You don't understand, Bapak. We'd do anything to protect our own tribe. If we didn't kill them, they may have killed us."

"That is not all," he continued. "We ate some of their flesh and drank some of their blood so that we would become stronger than they, following our traditions of 'sakti.'"

I nearly vomited at the thought. He started to cry as guilt and remorse set in. I was so sad for him. I said, "Son, you have placed a curse on yourself. You need to be delivered and set free from this terrible predicament. Jesus can definitely help you." And as we prayed with him and ministered to him on several occasions, he was delivered and set free from this curse. Today, he is a fine young man, married to one of our young ladies. Together they have two beautiful children. He still calls me regularly to see how we are doing. How blessed Kay and I are to have influenced their lives.

Like this young man, many tribal people have taken part in horrific rituals ordered by the witchdoctor or tribal chief. But there is hope. "Oh Jesus, set the Dayaks free from these demonic rituals. Deliver them and bring healing into their souls."

Nyunyu

During this horrible time of unrest on our island, a young man named Nyunyu was brought to our home by his older and younger brothers because he was seriously ill with typhoid. They were from the village called Kobuk, which belonged to the Matee tribe. For years we tried to plant a church in their village, but because of a strong occult presence, a church just never got off the ground. When Nyunyu arrived at our home, we immediately took him to the local hospital. After being in the hospital four days, we noticed that Nyunyu's stomach was swelling up profusely, and he seemed to be losing his mind. The doctor told us that his intestines had already started to perforate because of typhoid, and there was nothing more to do but take him back to his village and let him die. Of course that was not the news we wanted to hear. After all, all our children and leaders were praying for a miracle. Nyunyu's younger brother, Iyan, became so deeply concerned about his brother that he made the decision to give his life to the Lord right there in the hospital. However, his older brother Kimban, like Nyunyu, was a powerful member of the occult in their village. They were loyal followers of the witchdoctor and did everything he commanded. The people of their tribe lived in fear and darkness.

We decided our only option was to take Nyunyu to a surgeon at the general hospital in Pontianak, the capital of West Kalimantan. That was easier said than done. At the time, the Dayaks and the

Madurese were still fighting. Travelling on the roads was very dangerous. However, because the gracious hand of the Lord was upon us, some of our young men managed to get him to Pontianak in a small pickup truck with a mattress. At the hospital, the surgeon told us Nyunyu had a slim chance of survival, but he could operate. Nyunyu would need six pints of blood. Back then, there was no blood bank in the city. My leaders went from church to church asking for donors with the same blood type as our patient. After three days, six people stepped forward as potential donors. We discovered then that a number of Christians, usually young people, had a ministry of giving blood to those in need. When they gave, they would always present a testimony: they shared that long ago someone else gave His blood willingly to save them. His name is Jesus. Their ministry had a profound effect on people from other religions. Many came into the Kingdom of God as a result. The downside of their ministry was that many of them donated blood too often and ended up sick or even died. To them, though, this was a sacrifice they were willing to make. I was deeply humbled by their ministry.

Now that the surgeon had blood, he was able to operate on Nyunyu. The surgery took well over eight hours and was successful, according to the medical staff. Nyunyu, however, remained in a coma for several weeks. Every day, my young men would call to update me on his condition. They would weep on the phone, and not just for Nyunyu. Because every

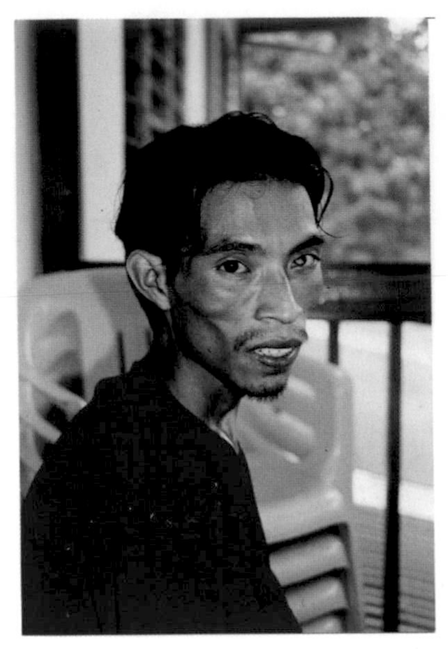

Nyunyu at the age of 25 weighing only 30 kilos, snatched from death and on the road to recovery. It is at this stage that he received Christ as his Lord and Savior.

Nyunyu now, totally healed and loving his new life with Jesus. What a miraculous change!

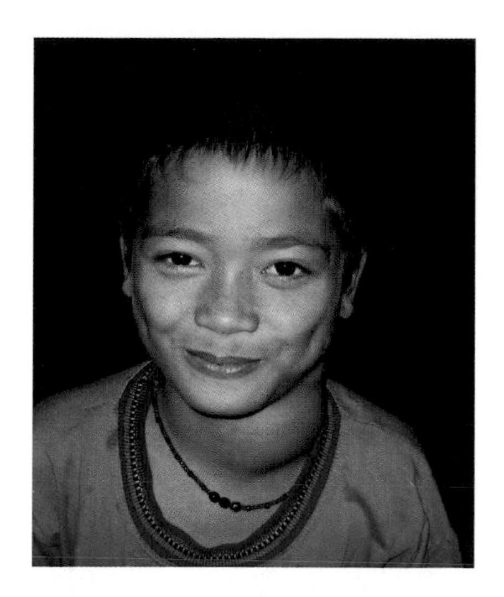

Left: *Tomi arrived with his brother Joni in 2007. Tomi was eight years old at the time and Joni, 11. Their father had already died, and their mother was mentally ill. She left them behind at a nearby village because they were both sick. The people of that village brought them to us as they were also too poor to care for them. Of course, we welcomed them into our home. After examining the boys at the local hospital, we discovered that Joni had tuberculosis. Tomi had cancer and needed chemotherapy. Joni received a 9-month treatment for tuberculosis and was healed after that time. Tomi needed specialist treatment so we made arrangements to get him a passport to take him to Kuching, Malaysia. There, they told us that he needed 13 treatments of chemotherapy worth USD15,000. We had no money but trusted the Lord for it and started with the first treatment. Many people prayed for him. Prior to his second chemo session, the entire cost for all his treatments was funded by a wonderful family in Singapore. What a blessing!*

Right: *Tomi now. Totally healed and walking with Jesus. He loves life, his new family, and school. Tomi and Joni will never forget what Jesus and people have done for them. In 2013 he was declared cancer free. Praise the Lord!*

room was occupied, Nyunyu's stretcher was in the hallway leading to the morgue. They saw many headless bodies that came in for disposal during the height of the tribal conflict. They were wheeled in every day, all day. Some belonged to young boys. It was unbearable. Oh, how I wish I could have jumped into my car and driven over there to support my young men, but the roads weren't safe. People were being stopped, beaten, and sometimes even burned alive in their cars. I encouraged my leaders to stay focused on the Lord. We were praying for them.

There was no nursing staff to look after Nyunyu so my guys had to stay with him and care for him. But they really had no idea how to do that. They didn't know that you had to massage a person in a coma and turn him regularly. I asked them to read Nyunyu the Word of God even though he was unconscious. They did that faithfully. After two weeks, Nyunyu emerged from his coma. Soon he was well enough to be discharged from the hospital. The chaos on the roads had subsided, and they came home. What a joyous time for us all! As Nyunyu walked in the door of our home, we were shocked to see how frail and malnourished he looked. He weighed only 30 kilos (about 66 pounds), but he had a sparkle in his eyes. He asked what he must do to receive this Jesus he had heard of. He then shared his experience with us.

He said, "Before my brothers brought me to your place here, I had this strange dream. In my dream I saw this bare green hill in the distance from

my village. It was the strangest sight because the hills around us all had trees, but this one had no trees. It just had a wooden cross on top. As I looked at this strange sight a voice said to me, 'Nyunyu, follow me.' I had no idea who it was or what it really meant. I woke up and pondered the meaning of this dream. I knew that this cross may have something to do with the little church down the road in the next village, but I was told not to mix with them. Meanwhile, my illness got worse day by day. The witchdoctor's medicines and potions didn't seem to work. My brothers finally decided to take me to you, Pak Ronny. The next thing I remember is lying on a bed, but I could not move or open my eyes. I kept on hearing someone standing close to me talking to me as if he were reading something. All of a sudden I heard the following words read: *Then Jesus said to His disciples, "If any of you wants to be my follower, you must put aside your selfish ambition, shoulder your cross, and follow me" (Matthew 16:24).* The words 'cross' and 'follow me' jumped out. I realized it was Jesus who in that dream had instructed me to pick up my cross and follow Him. I remember next waking up from my coma. I was incredibly weak and frail. Still, it was as if I was zapped with something that made me determined to fight and get healthy again quickly. And here I am now, asking you what I must do to receive and follow this Jesus. I know I should have been dead by now, but this Jesus has awakened me and healed me. I want to follow Him."
We praised God for the incredible transformation in

his life. Not only did he recover physically but he also found a new, abundant life in Christ. He was a new creation.

Six months later, when his health had been totally restored, I took him to visit his village. Everyone was astonished to see that Nyunyu was not just alive, but so radiant. His face glowed. Nyunyu shared what God the Creator had done in his life. He spoke in his own tribal language so all the women and children also could understand. Many people came forward and gave their lives to the Lord, including all his family. Many people who had been loyal followers of the witchdoctor also became Christians. The breakthrough was an answer to many years of prayer. What an incredible testimony of God's grace! And we felt the difference. Before this miracle, you could just feel the presence of darkness covering the entire area. But after the breakthrough, the blanket of evil disappeared. Today, when we enter the region it is as if heaven has opened above the area. How awesome! Nyunyu is serving the Lord now in his village. His older brother, Kimban, is a pastor and has such a loving and passionate ministry to his own people. What an incredible change occurs when people respond as God reveals Himself.

Maneuvering for Medicine

At one time we had a number of girls who had contracted malaria and needed hospital treatment. Nurses don't look after the basic needs of patients, so many family members stay with the patient around the clock in the hospital. In this case that was us, of course. So a number of our older girls took turns caring for the younger ones.

We had four girls in the hospital who all needed malaria medication. However, every chemist in town, including the hospital chemist, had run out of malaria medicine. This was particularly upsetting because I knew that the World Health Organization distributes all sorts of "difficult to get" medications for the poor. But often it gets into the wrong hands and the poor miss out. Frustrated, I told a hospital nurse that I don't understand how a place like this can possibly run out of malaria medicine since it is such a problem here. She then pulled me aside; she looked to the left and right to make sure nobody was watching us. She then opened her fist. It was full of malaria medication. She asked if this was what I needed. I was astounded. "Yes, it is! Where did you get it?" She didn't answer, but gave me the price. It was almost three times the normal cost. I didn't argue with her out of fear that she may back out and then I wouldn't have any medicine for our girls. However, from that day on, I knew how the system worked.

Understanding that system certainly helped us months later. We brought a young man who was very sick with typhoid to the hospital. The doctor prescribed all sorts of medication. I had to buy it from the hospital chemist or one of the chemists in town. After a few hours, I had acquired three days' worth. I put it all into a bag, and placed it into the drawer of his bedside table, a rickety old wooden box. One of our boys stayed with the young man to care for him throughout the night. I left at 10pm and returned in the morning to discover that all the medication was gone. I asked various people about it, and they professed to know nothing. Finally a nurse informed me that all his medication was finished, and I needed to purchase more. Well I knew I bought enough for three days, and I knew how the system worked. So I stepped into the nurses' room. It was full of people. One of the male nurses told me to wait outside because they were changing shifts and discussing patient matters.

"That is good timing then," I declared, "since I need to speak to all of you."

They were not amused, and if looks could kill, I would be dead.

"I was told that all the medication I bought yesterday for one of our young men is already used up. So I just want to ask all of you if anyone has misplaced it or put it somewhere else."

Once again, the answer I got was that it was already finished.

"In that case," I stated, "I am here to tell you that I will go shopping now. In half an hour I will be back, and all his medication had better be back in his drawer, or you will have a problem with me."

They could see by my expression and body language that I meant business. And sure enough, when I got back half an hour later, the missing medicine was back in his drawer. Praise the Lord, the message got through. Now they know never to mess with me or any of our children.

A few days later, as we were caring for our girls in the hospital, a female doctor walked up to me. She obviously had heard about the incident with the nurses, and confronted me, "Why do you care about these girls anyway? What are they to you?" Her sarcastic tone underscored her disdain for the local people who were of a different race.

"And who might you be?" I replied, knowing full well who she was.

"I am the doctor here," she answered.

"And why did you become a doctor?" I asked.

"For the money, of course," she said, insinuating that the answer was obvious.

"Really?" I said. "Shame on you. Didn't you become a doctor because you wanted to help people?"

"Doctors become doctors here to become rich," she said with a smirk.

I was so annoyed with her. "You really need God in your life," I said. "Why don't you come to our church?"

She didn't like my question, so she walked away.

However, a few weeks later, guess who turned up at our church? The doctor! During the whole service, she stood in the back with her arms folded. She left before the meeting was over, so we didn't get to speak to her. I didn't think she would come back, but to our astonishment, she turned up again the following Sunday, and the week after that. I think it was the fourth Sunday when she came forward and asked the Lord into her life. Wow! Obviously God was working in her heart all along in a big way even though it was not noticeable in her outward expression. We had been praying for her all along, but we really thought that she would be a difficult person to lead to Christ. Months later, I asked her, "What made you decide to become a Christian?" She said, "You people here practice what you preach. You don't just tell people how they should live, but you actually do it yourselves. I have seen you all at the hospital. You really love and care for people even though they are not your family or your people. I don't know how you can do it, but you do. So it must be this Jesus you know. I want to be like that too. I want to help and care for people like Jesus does and like you do."

Most days she would visit just to talk about God. She had so many questions about her new life. A few weeks later she came to us very distressed. She told us that she could no longer work as a doctor at the hospital because its system was so corrupt. All the employees had to follow along. If you didn't, you'd get fired. She could no longer dishonor God by working in such a system. However, I told her to look at it differently: Yes, you cannot be corrupt, but God did not place you there without a plan. You are His light there now, so there must be a way for you to continue to do your job without following corrupt behavior. I asked her to pray and seek God for an answer, and we would do likewise. A little over a week later, she burst into our place. She said that she had found a way! Every so often, the World Health Organization provides hospitals with loads of expensive medication, particularly for TB, HIV, malaria, typhoid, and vitamin A, etc. These medicines are expensive but supposed to be given free of charge to the poor. Problem was, as soon as the hospital got its allocation, it was often either confiscated and then sold to the highest bidder, or the poor had to pay for it. Well, our doctor devised her own way of making sure the poor received the medicine they needed: after examining her patient, she would hand him or her a prescription and an envelope. She would slip her own money in the envelope so the patient could purchase the medicine from the chemist. Needless to say, she didn't have much left for herself to live on, but it didn't seem to be an issue for her. She desired so much to serve Jesus. She became a light to a people desperately in need of Christ.

In the Heart of Borneo

One day, we made plans to visit a particular tribe to see how we could minister to its people. (This is the same tribe where a terrible atrocity happened a few years later: While the husbands of the village were working in the jungle, their women and children had their heads, hands, and feet cut off by some angry mob seeking revenge.) On this day, we packed our supplies and drove as far as the roads could take us. When we stopped to look over our plans for the day, suddenly a man appeared. He was a tribal chief. We did not know him, but he insisted we go to his village. Now you must understand that in the jungle, it is risky business to go with a stranger, for one never knows what will happen. Some tribes living in remote regions are still very primitive and can be hostile. I certainly did not want to end up in someone's soup. But I felt the Holy Spirit telling me that we should set aside our original plan and go with this man. I was still a little reluctant. I was not completely sure if this was the prompting of the Lord or just my own adventurous spirit.

I agreed to go with him, and one of my young men offered to travel with me. The chief was very clear. "I want you to come to our village and tell us this news you have."

The chief led us to his little canoe, with a 2HP engine in the rear. The boat was so narrow I could hardly fit my backside into it, and I am not very large. We started out on the large river, but soon turned down a smaller river through the tangled growth of some jungle trees. After a considerable distance, he turned again into an even smaller stream where we had to get out and push. We meandered through a web of waterways, streams, and, occasionally, into a larger river. This journey continued for two to three hours. I was completely lost and, frankly, a little nervous as to how this trip was going to end. Did I really believe that the Holy Spirit wanted me to go? "Who are these people anyway, God? Do they know anything at all about You? What do You want me to share with them? They are animists. They believe in spirits everywhere and are heavily influenced by their witchdoctors. I can't just open the Bible and proclaim, 'Jesus the Lamb of God Who takes away the sins of the world!' These people have never seen a lamb and wouldn't even know what I was talking about. I have to use picture forms, things they can relate to in their village and surroundings, but I haven't a clue what to say. God, I didn't prepare for this to happen today. Please help me. I don't want to die. I still want to do so many things for You. God, where are You?" I was losing my nerve. Me, a man of great faith? Yeah, right.

Huge trees hung over the river; it resembled a dark eerie tunnel. Suddenly, large idols appeared on both sides of the waterway. Some were carved trees. Others were piles of rocks with faces painted on them, with fire burning underneath. It was scary. I was ready to suggest that we turn around and head back to our car. But the chief pressed on, and the little 2HP engine continued purring.

We entered a creek blanketed with jungle overgrowth. Then suddenly, the creek opened to a beautiful small lake. It was so calm and picturesque. Looking across the lake, I could see many huts. People stood on the shore, waving excitedly.

I told the chief, “Look, the people are obviously expecting you.”

He said, “No, they’re expecting *you*.”

“How can this be?” I asked. “I didn’t even know until a few hours ago that I would be coming here. How could they possibly be expecting *me*?”

“Ah, news like this travels fast in these jungles,” replied the chief.

I wasn’t sure if this was good news or bad news. I kept looking straight ahead to see if I could see a huge pot on the fire prepared for my demise, but praise the Lord, there wasn’t any.

The people were so excited and kind. Many of the women and children had never seen White Man before so they kept staring. I am not sure what they thought, but judging from their expression, they probably didn’t think I was handsome.

People from other tribes rushed over when they heard about this meeting. Someone was going to tell them about another spirit they knew nothing about. They all came and sat down on the ground. The crowd numbered in the hundreds. The chief motioned for all to be quiet.

"You," he said pointing to me, "come now, and speak."

Honestly, at this moment, I realized I had two choices. One was run for my life. But run where? I didn't even know where I was, so that wasn't a real option. Two, just go to the front and tell them. Tell them what and how? God hadn't given me a picture yet, nothing that would help these people relate to what I wanted to say.

"God, I believe You didn't bring me here without reason, so please help me now." Then I prayed, "Okay, Holy Spirit, I am taking Your hand now, trusting that You will give me what I need to get the job done. Thank You, Lord."

And as I took the first step, God gave me a mental picture of what to say. I learned something that day. God does not push, shove, or pull us into obedience. He just asks us and waits until we take the first step. Taking the first step means saying, "Okay, God, I may not understand this, and I may not know what to do, but I trust in You and know that You are here with me to help me." And as we take the first step in obedience, God then gives us all we need: His power, His words, His provision, and His resources to complete the task He sets before us.

I walked out to the front and didn't even introduce myself. I launched straight into what I had to say. "There is a Great Spirit Who has created the heavens and the earth, and you and me. Just imagine that He is over there." With my hand I pointed to the sky to my left. "Now you can't see Him, but He's here, and He loves us immensely. He created us so that He can have fellowship with us, a relationship. We are His children and He wants the best for us. He is like a Father to us. He represents love, health, goodness, happiness, joy, eternal life, and everything that is good. There is no sin in Him. There is no other spirit like Him. All He wants is that we desire to know Him and to embrace Him.

There is, however, another spirit present, the evil spirit. Just imagine he is over there." I motioned to the sky to my right. "He represents death, war, disease, jealousy, hatred, and all sin. Now when we bow down to the spirit of the trees and the spirit of the rivers, the rocks, the sun, the harvest, or every other thing, we actually are bowing down to this evil spirit, and we have our backs turned to the Great Spirit Who created us. This Great Spirit grieves immensely because we are worshipping the evil spirit instead of Him Who created us."

The people were stunned at this revelation. You could tell on their faces. They were silent. I continued, "This God, the Great Spirit, loves us so much that He sent His one and only Son to die for our sins. This Son paid the price for our sins. That's how much He loves us. He did this so that we could be forgiven of our sins and come into fellowship with Him. As we embrace His Son, Jesus, we are embracing the Great Spirit." They looked horrified. They knew what sacrifices were. They made them every day to appease their spirits. They would even leave food at the bottom of the tree for the spirit of the tree instead of feeding their hungry children. They were afraid that if they didn't sacrifice to these spirits, there would be horrendous consequences. They lived in constant fear. If their child became sick or died, they believed it was their fault because they didn't sacrifice enough to the spirit of life. If their rice crop failed, they believed it was their fault because they didn't sacrifice enough to the spirit of the harvest. They woke up each morning wondering what mood the spirits would be in on that particular day. When they went to sleep at night, they wondered if the spirits had accepted their offerings. On top of that, the witchdoctors put even more fear into their lives with all their rituals and superstitions. Can you imagine living life this way?

I continued to speak, "Many years ago, someone told me about this Great Spirit and His love for me, so I made the choice to put my trust in Him, embracing Him and turning away from all other spirits. My life was completely changed. So today, you too have the opportunity to turn your back on all these evil spirits you've been worshipping, and receive the Great Spirit Who loves you. You cannot add this Great Spirit to your collection of spirits. You must either worship Him or them, one or the other. You cannot worship both. If you want to worship this Great Spirit and do away with all the others, then I invite you to come forward, and I will pray with you."

I was not prepared for what transpired next. Half of the people stood, ran forward, and fell before me. They wept, and some cried out loud, saying, "Oh, Great Spirit, we did not know we were not allowed to do these things. We did not know you existed. Please forgive us." People wailed with remorse. I honestly didn't know what to do. I couldn't do anything. I felt numb. I just stood back and stared and cried with them as the Holy Spirit was touching and working in their hearts. As I stood there, I realized suddenly that I could have missed this opportunity. I could have said to the chief who came for me that I was too busy on that day. After all, I had already made other plans. But praise God, I obeyed the prompting of the Holy Spirit. If I hadn't, perhaps all this would not have happened. The people were ready to hear the good news. All they needed was someone to come over and share the Gospel message of love and salvation so that they, too, could be saved. That was all. A church was birthed that day in that little village deep in the jungle of Borneo. After a few weeks, we sent a couple of workers to help the people understand the Christian faith. Since then that church has grown and started other congregations with the surrounding tribes and villages.

The ride back in the canoe was a time for me to reflect and pray. All the people needed was to hear the Gospel message of God's love. How many thousands of villages still have not heard? They, too, need someone to come and share the good news. They're living in fear and superstition, and they will die in that darkness if someone doesn't go and tell them. It is the same wherever we are, really. How many people where we live are just waiting for someone to tell them there is hope? Sure, some could care less about God, but there are others who need to hear the Gospel from someone who cares.

By the time we got to our car, my burden for missions had grown a thousand fold. That's why I'm restless: every day is important to me because it is one more day to tell people about Jesus. God, help me not to waste time!

Paul for Sale?

On a visit to one of the villages, I decided to take our 12-year-old son, Paul. We were invited to the opening ceremony of a newly-built longhouse. It was a joyous occasion. The people honored and thanked God for the resources to build a new home for more than 40 families. The celebrations continued for days. On one of those days, Paul and I were sitting opposite the tribal chief. He kept staring at Paul; Paul felt uncomfortable. Then out of the blue the chief pointed to him and asked me, "How much do you want for that?"

I thought he was referring to a shell necklace that Paul was wearing around his neck. It had a shark's tooth on it.

I said, "I am not sure if he wants to sell that."

The chief looked rather annoyed. He said, "You are the father, yes? Well then, how much do you want for him?"

"You mean my son?" I asked. "You want to buy my *son*?"

I thought that was the biggest joke I'd heard in a long time.

Paul asked me what he said.

"Hang on a minute, Paul," I said, "we are negotiating here. He wants to buy you."

Paul grabbed my arm. He looked worried.

I turned to him, "I wonder how many pigs you are worth." Paul thumped me one.

I faced the tribal chief, "Now why would you want to buy my son?"

I had to admit that he was a good looking lad, but I was very curious why he would possibly want Paul.

"For my daughter in marriage," stated the chief.

My mouth dropped. I realized that I had better be careful what I said because after all, we were in a very different culture. Some customs are completely foreign and weird to us, yet very serious. So I quickly dismissed the idea and responded firmly, "He is not for sale."

Oh my goodness! Can you imagine Paul marrying at the age of 12 to who knows who? We joked about it many times afterward. And every now and then, especially when Paul was misbehaving, I still threatened to negotiate a price with the tribal chief if he didn't correct his ways. Oh, how our cultures differ!

Sumar

We often sent our young church planters into the jungle, sometimes two by two and sometimes alone, to travel systematically from village to village, to share the story of God's love. Some villages were on hilltops; usually, they were close to a river or creek. Some tribes welcomed our church planters with open arms; others would tell them to leave or risk being killed.

One of our young church planters is named Sumar. He set out with his backpack strapped to his shoulders and his Bible in hand. Many of the villagers he encountered wanted nothing to do with the message he was sharing. They told him to leave immediately or else. He would shake the dust or mud off his sandals and continue his journey from one place to another. One day, after a considerable hike, he was walking down a steep slope. He saw in the distance a few huts among the giant trees. Then he spotted an old lady heading toward him. She was screaming and waving her hands hysterically. His first reaction was, "Oh boy, demon possession." But when she reached Sumar, she embraced him. Once she quieted down, she said, "I knew you would come." Apparently, years before, someone from another tribe told her that there was a Great Spirit who loves the tribes so much that He sent His Son to die for us so that our sins could be forgiven. She learned that He was called the Spirit of the Christians but she had no idea who or what they were. From that day on, she decided to worship and pray to this spirit too.

She was an animist and believed objects had spirits. She worshipped and sacrificed to the spirit of the river, the trees, the rocks, and many other spirits. Now she was also including the Christian Spirit in her daily prayer and worship. Even though she knew nothing about Him, she would say, “Christian Spirit, You need to send somebody to tell us about You so we can know You.” For years, she kept telling the village folks, “You will see. One day, this Great Spirit will send a messenger to make Himself known to us.” When she saw Sumar coming down the hill through the trees, she knew that the messenger had arrived. She was so excited. She grabbed him by the arm and led him into the village going from hut to hut, telling everybody that he had arrived. There, in that remote location, the people gathered to listen intently to the message of God’s love and the sacrifice of Christ. The people were amazed and receptive to the Gospel. Within weeks, most of the people gave their lives to the Lord. A marvelous Christian church was born among the Ribun tribe in that wild jungle. Weeks later, we managed to place two Christian workers there from another ministry, since ours didn’t have anyone left to serve long term. Through daily discipleship, we saw the Holy Spirit transform the lives of the new believers. Soon they were planting churches. The people quickly learned their responsibility to share the good news with other tribes around them.

Ratna

A great problem for the local people is the influence of the witchdoctors. They have a powerful impact on the tribes in every way and in every village. They claim that they are able to communicate with the spirit world. Where there is ignorance regarding diseases and medical treatment, magical ceremonies and pretensions to supernatural powers are allowed full sway. Fear and anxiety make the tribal people eager to believe in any suggested remedy, however absurd it may be. The witchdoctor's function is to defeat and drive away the malignant spirits that cause sickness and death. In our work among the tribes, it is the witchdoctor who often is most resistant to our presence. He does not want his power or authority questioned. In our work among the tribes, it is often the witchdoctor who reacts to our presence. Some have been converted, though not many.

One particular case involving witchdoctors comes to mind. When we arrived at a village of the Matee tribe, we were met by one of the tribesmen who had recently given his life to the Lord. We hurried to his hut where his nine-year-old daughter, Ratna, was very sick. His home was filled with various village people. We were startled to find Ratna dehydrated. She was having frequent convulsions. Her father said she had been in this condition for four days. We prayed and prayed for this little girl. "Ratna, child of the Most High God, be healed in

Jesus' Name." One of the tribesmen in the house, unbeknown to us, was the local witchdoctor. He was observing everything we did. We suspected that Ratna had meningitis and needed urgent medical treatment in a hospital. That was out of the question though. There were no hospitals in the area. The girl was burning up with a high fever. We had to get her temperature down quickly. Because it was the dry season, there was no water for a bath. The only water they had was in a hole outside which the people had dug for bathing. However, the water was green. Still, it was water, and it was a bit cool, so we carried the girl and plunged her into the disgusting green water. Her temperature dropped fast, but she was still terribly dehydrated and needed urgent IV therapy. She couldn't eat or drink. Later that day, we found out that there was a small clinic about two hours away. Her father was very reluctant to take her because he thought people always die in hospitals. "This is often true," I told him, "but only because you people decide to take the patient to the hospital when it is already too late. Your little girl needs urgent treatment now so don't wait any longer." When we arrived at the clinic, a medical student happened to be there. That was an answer to our prayer. Often, these clinics in the jungle are unmanned. No one wants to be posted in those remote wild places. But praise God, someone was there to treat Ratna. She was on an intravenous drip for a few hours, but then the father insisted he must take her home. He feared his daughter would die in the clinic. We tried very hard to convince him that Ratna needed to stay. He refused to listen. In the end, we took him and Ratna back to their village, but continued to keep her on the intravenous drip. Because we had to go back home ourselves, we had arranged for the medical student to check on the girl regularly. We paid for his expenses in advance. Thankfully, he followed through on his promise, something that isn't always done if you are not there yourself for accountability.

Two weeks later, we came back. Ratna was walking around, smiling, and enjoying life again. It was so good to see her healed and playing with her friends. How we rejoiced in our Lord. However, on our next visit, we were shocked to see Ratna back in a terrible state again, worse than when we saw her the first time. This time, however, she was surrounded by the witchdoctor's paraphernalia. It was around her on the floor, sprinkled over her, and hanging above her.

I said to her father, "What have you done? Why on earth did you bring the witchdoctor in? I thought you were a Christian putting your faith in Jesus."

"It wasn't me," he said. "It was my father. He brought his own village witchdoctor."

"This child is yours," I replied. "God gave her to you, not to your father, to care for. I know you must respect your parents and elders, but not at the cost of disobeying God and losing your child. You are responsible for her. You must choose who you are going to follow, Jesus or the witchdoctor."

We left without praying for her, which made me feel terrible, but we knew that the father had to make a choice. A lot was at stake here. A few hours later, we came back. We felt relieved to see all of the witchdoctor's paraphernalia heaped outside, ready to burn. The father came outside and declared that he had made his choice. "I follow Jesus," he said. "Ratna is mine. I am responsible for her. I know I have to deal with my father. He may not understand at first, but hopefully he will eventually." We burned all the stuff, prayed, and renounced all the demonic words spoken over Ratna, then went inside to pray for her. The house was still full of people. There was also a witchdoctor, unknown to us. He was not the witchdoctor who performed all the rituals over Ratna but the local witchdoctor. It turns out that he marveled when we prayed and laid our hands on her. He pondered the origin of this power. Weeks later, when we came back for a few days, we were having coffee in our church building. The local witchdoctor suddenly ran in and waved his arms frantically, motioning for to us to follow him. We did. We realized that we were entering the witchdoctor's house. There was stuff everywhere, including grotesque demonic carvings. He pointed to a room. We weren't sure what to expect, but there in the bedroom was a young girl who had the same symptoms as Ratna, though less severe. He said, "I saw what you did with Ratna. Now I want you to use your power on my daughter." We didn't say anything to the witchdoctor. We simply laid our hands on his daughter and said, "Little girl, in the name of Jesus Christ, be healed." Nothing seemed to happen. We told her father that we were having a service that evening, and he and his family were invited to come. We could see from his facial expression that he was not interested. After all, his little girl was not healed.

That evening, after a great praise and worship time, we invited our guest speaker to share from the Word of God. The preacher knew nothing about the incident with the witchdoctor but the message was, "Who will you follow, Jesus or the witchdoctor?" On one occasion, I looked toward the back of the little church building, and to my surprise, I saw the witchdoctor standing in the doorway with his wife and children. His little girl was there; she was no longer sick! The speaker preached a powerful sermon. At the conclusion, people had an opportunity to respond. "If you want to receive this Jesus into your life and do away with your belief in the witchdoctor, then come forward now and we will pray with you." To everyone's amazement, the witchdoctor was the first one to step forward with his whole family and receive Christ! You should have seen the reaction on the faces of the crowd. That became the talk of the region. The witchdoctor had become an ambassador for Jesus. It didn't take long before he was helping us plant other churches, sharing about how powerful our God is - more powerful than any witchdoctor!

Mandis

When we found Mandis in the jungle, he was about seven years old. He came from the Koli village which belongs to the Matee tribe. He suffered from severe malnutrition which is common among tribes living a long distance from the road system. People living on or near any road or major river are often much better off, since they can trade with others. On the other hand, those living in remote regions away from any road or river lack the opportunity to trade for food and other necessities of life.

We took Mandis to the medical doctor at a local hospital. The doctor determined that the little boy was very sick. His kidneys were not functioning properly as a result of severe malnutrition for many years. We were instructed to put Mandis on a strict diet. Under no circumstances was Mandis allowed to return home to his remote village, as the diet would kill him. The doctor prescribed medication, and we made our way home. However, after several months, his condition worsened. We secured a passport and took him to kidney specialist Dr. Simon Wong, a wonderful Christian brother at the Timberland Hospital in Kuching. After examining Mandis, Dr. Wong said his condition was serious but not life threatening. However, he couldn't be sure until he performed a biopsy on his kidney. The tests had to be analyzed in Kuala Lumpur since Kuching lacked the proper facilities. After the biopsy, we received more medication and went back home. After a few weeks Dr. Wong asked us to come back to Kuching. He had gotten the biopsy results. The prognosis: Mandis' condition was more critical than the doctor anticipated. He may have six months to a few years before he would need dialysis or a kidney transplant. Neither was an option to us in our very remote area of Borneo. "What he needs is a miracle," Dr. Wong said. He gave us more medicine and said he and his church would pray for a miracle. We left for home discouraged but knew that God could do anything as we witnessed many times before.

For the next few years, we faithfully kept Mandis to a strict diet and his medicine. His health fluctuated. We had to make several follow-up visits to Dr. Wong in Kuching.

Shortly after, when I returned from a ministry trip to Holland, I was amazed at a tremendous improvement in Mandis' health. I said, "Son, you look so good. You look as if you are healed." His first words to me were, "Dad, I feel wonderful! I have never felt so good in my life." We rejoiced together. That day, I kept on thinking how wonderful Mandis was looking. I thanked God for the change that had occurred in such a short time. Once I greeted everyone at home and caught up on the latest news, I went to my office to peruse all the mail that had accumulated in my absence.

One letter was from a lady who lived in Benalla, Australia. Ever since she read about Mandis in our newsletter years ago, she had been praying for him every day. "At a recent Sunday morning service, a visiting pastor with a healing ministry was bringing us the Word of the Lord," she wrote. "After he finished preaching, he invited all the sick to come forward for prayer. Then the pastor said, 'If you know of someone who is ill but not present with us this morning, you come forward on their behalf and we will pray and believe together for Jesus to heal that person.' I immediately decided to go to the front on behalf of Mandis, the boy in the children's home in Borneo. Ronny, as this man put his hand on my head and started to pray for Mandis, it was as if a lightning bolt went through me, and I just knew that Mandis was healed. And so I just wanted to ask you how Mandis is right now?" As I was reading this my eyes filled up with tears. I had goose bumps all over. I kept thinking what I told Mandis just a few hours before, "Son, you look so good. You look as if you are healed."

I replied to her letter, reporting that God had answered her prayers. Mandis is healed and well. Recent medical exams confirmed that his kidneys are functioning normally. At the time of this writing, Mandis is 20 years old. He finished high school, and plans to enroll in the university to study architecture. What an awesome God we have!

Witchdoctor in Mayan

A short time later, we were on our way to visit another village belonging to the Matee tribe for a few days. We had a YWAM (Youth with a Mission) team with us who had come over to help us out for a few weeks. They were great. We had a wonderful time ministering to the tribal people. As we were about to leave, their witchdoctor came up to me and asked,

"Do you have some power medicine for my leg? It is in excruciating pain." He had a massive boil just above his knee. I knew it had to be lanced as I have had boils myself before. I had my medical box with me but no surgical knife. The only thing I had was a huge syringe and needle which would do just fine to open the boil. When he saw it, he started to freak out. People here do not like needles of any kind. They are afraid of them. I reassured him that this boil had to be opened up to alleviate the pressure, and this was the only way. He looked very worried, but I could see in his eyes that he trusted me. We prayed for him, asking the Lord to heal him completely. Next, I gave him a piece of wood to bite. I instructed him to look the other way. As I pierced the boil, nothing happened. I had to pierce it a dozen times to get a big enough hole. Finally it ruptured so we could clean the infection. Some members of the YWAM team had to hold the guy down. Afterward, I gave him antibiotics and told him to finish the course as prescribed even if he already felt much better. Often, when we give people antibiotics for five to seven days, they stop after three days when they feel much better. They like to bless their fellow tribal people with the leftovers: one tablet for Grandma because she has a headache, one for their uncle because he is coughing a lot, two for their child because he has worms, and two for their brother because he was drunk. They find it so difficult and wasteful to finish the whole course when they are feeling better.

Weeks later, when I returned to this

witchdoctor to see how he was, he ran to greet me. He couldn't wait to show me his leg. It was all healed. He said that he almost passed out when I poked the boil with the syringe. And if not for the piece of wood I gave him to bite on, he would have cried like a baby.

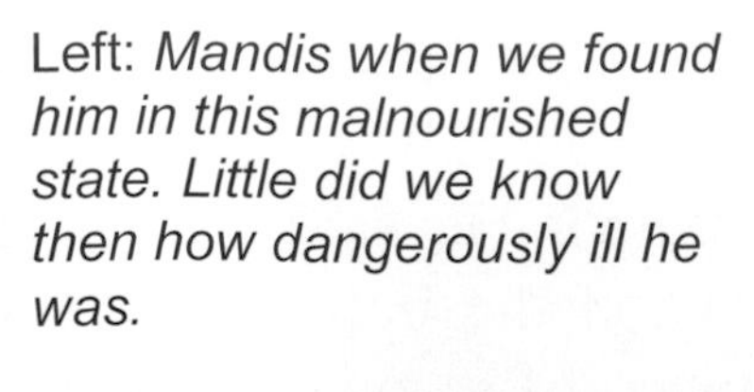

Left: *Mandis when we found him in this malnourished state. Little did we know then how dangerously ill he was.*

Right: *Mandis a few years later, full of life and making the most of every day.*

Left: *Mandis now, miraculously healed. He finished high school and loves life. Grateful to his huge family at Living Waters Village and very grateful to the Lord for rescuing him, healing him, and blessing him with an abundant life.*

One of the tribal huts belonging to the Mualang tribe.

Above: *A longhouse belonging to the Iban tribe. About 30-50 families live in such a building. Each family has its own section in the building, with the huge verandah for all sorts of communal activities.*

Left: *A mother and her child from the village called Telogah which belongs to the Matee tribe.*

The New Vision

All of us at New Hope Ministries served the Lord together as a team for more than four years. As a result of much conversation, times of prayer, good times and not so good times, we concluded it was time for us to separate. We decided to go deeper into the jungle, closer to unreached tribes. Where exactly, we didn't know. After 40 days of praying and fasting, desperately wanting to know His will in the matter, I felt the Holy Spirit saying to go to Sintang where He would show us the next step to take.

We were out of money because we had invested everything we had into the ministry at Sanggau. We built our home and some of the buildings for the children. But God made it very clear that He wanted us to build a home for 1,000 children and youth in crisis, and a school for 2,000. I held this vision in my heart for three days before sharing it with Kay. "Let's do it," she said. I was a bit apprehensive sharing our vision with others as people may have misunderstood our motive. We were not trying to outdo other missionary work in our area. Kay and I were convinced that the vision was from God. We separated ourselves from the ministry at Sanggau, rented a building in another town deeper in the jungle, and soon, more than 100 children filled our home. The idea of a thousand children in our children's home thrilled us. But building a school for 2,000 children was a task I did not cherish. In fact, I dreaded it. Remember, I was kicked out of school at age 16. School was not a favorite subject with me. So it was time to have another serious talk with God.

"God, if you are expecting me to build a home for 1,000 children, and a school for 2,000, I will need a large piece of land. It will have to be at least 25 hectares (the equivalent of 60 acres). We will need road access (which almost does not exist in the jungle). It must be serviced with public electricity (again a rarity in the jungle). It must have river access, springs providing fresh, clean drinking water, and be at a high enough elevation so that there won't be a flood every time it rains. Oh yes, God, and it must be dirt cheap."

I knew what He wanted. He now knew what I needed.

And so the search began. As soon as the local people heard that a White Man wanted to buy some land, many people came forward with land for our consideration. Buying land is a very risky business here. You must show respect; you cannot in any way mistakenly imply you have a deal. If they perceive you had agreed to buy their land, and you failed to follow through on the transaction, your life would be in danger. People literally lose their heads from misunderstandings in real estate transactions. In our search, we traveled by boat, canoe, car, motorbike, and any mode of transportation available. For months, we reviewed so many pieces of property that we were starting to become discouraged. However, after receiving a dream from the Lord to look for land across the river, the search continued with vigor.

Our quest took us near the town where we had rented the temporary site for our children's home. Two pieces of property across the river Kapuas seemed quite attractive. The first question we asked was, "Does it flood during the rainy season?" The immediate response was always, "Oh, never!" We visited one piece of land three times. The third time, we walked the border on one side, and I noticed an old man standing near a tree in the distance. He was all by himself observing the scene. How odd, I thought. As the land owners tried to persuade us to buy their land, I excused myself to walk over and greet this old man by the tree.

Out of the blue, he said, "This is the other border."

"I know," I said, "and I have been told that it never floods here. Is that correct?"

He said, "Oh yes, it *does*, up to here," pointing to his forehead.

"No, those guys there say it never floods here," I replied. "I cannot see any evidence of any previous flooding either."

Again he pointed to his forehead indicating how high the flood waters would rise. "Not often, but sometimes up to here."

Well, sometimes is not good enough for me. It must never flood. Amazed, I thanked him and returned to the land owners.

"You are wrong," I asserted. "It does flood here at times and quite a bit. Why are you saying that it never floods?"

They repeated their claim that it never floods here.

"Guys, you're not telling me the truth. I just spoke with that old man over there by the tree. He said it does flood, sometimes up to here," I gestured to my forehead.

"What old man?" one of them asked.

I turned around. There was no old man. He vanished. Could he have been one of God's angels sent to protect us from making a deal? The conversation ended, and our search continued. Thank You, Jesus, for keeping us from making a bad mistake.

Another local group of land owners approached us, but the property failed to meet many of our requirements. However, I was a little impatient and thought it might be okay. There were certain aspects of the property that we could change, and we could tell ourselves that maybe this was the property that God wanted us to buy. However, one important matter needed to be resolved, and that was the cost. We met on four different occasions with the tribal people, trying to decide the price. We then agreed to two and a half million Rupiah (USD250 per hectare), and we were ready to sign the contract. The plan was to meet with our legal counselor and complete the deal the next Saturday.

But one of the elders of this tribe showed up for the meeting. I hadn't met him previously, yet he immediately took charge of the conversation. "You can buy the property," he stated, "but the price will be two and a half *billion* Rupiah per hectare (USD250,000 per hectare)." I laughed because I thought he was joking, but his expression was very serious.

"Sir, we've already agreed on the price," I said, "and it's only one-thousandth of the amount that you're demanding! The price is two and a half *million*, not billion."

He was agitated at our refusal to accept the higher price. Well, I wasn't pleased with the sudden turn of events. I said that I was no longer interested, and if he could sell it to someone else for that price, then he should go ahead.

The conversation ended with him insisting that there would be no sale unless we agreed to his price.

"Totally right," I said. "Definitely no sale with me."

The local tribal people were furious. They were angry at the elder for disrupting the sale, and they were mad at us for not paying the higher price. We left speedily because we knew that our lives were in jeopardy. We had broken our agreement to buy, and jungle justice was about to take over. We thanked the Lord again for saving us.

Our search continued. After ten months, I was becoming very impatient with God. One night, lying in bed with Kay, I was reading Psalm 37. I came to verse 34, "*Don't be impatient for the Lord to act. Travel steadily along His path. He will honor you, giving you the land ...*" Kay looked at me and quietly said, "See, be patient. God is at work." I responded by asking God and Kay to forgive me for my impatience. I kissed Kay goodnight, and we went peacefully to sleep.

Two to three days later, the phone rang. "Are you the man looking for land?" asked the voice on the other end.

"Yes," I replied, "I'm looking for land."

"Well, I have land," he announced.

"Oh, great!" I thought. This is the 50th or so phone call from someone who wants to sell their land.

"If you will meet me at the coffee shop in Nanga Pinoh at 11am Monday, I'll show you the property. It's near the telecom tower."

After driving three hours, I turned up at the appointed time and place in front of the coffee shop. An older man came out, got into my car, and directed, "My land is that way." The road straight ahead was riddled with potholes so huge they could swallow an entire vehicle. It took us one hour just to go ten kilometers. Eventually, I asked him, "Where is the telecom tower? I thought you said your land was near the telecom tower."

"No, I never said that," he said.

"Yes, you did," I reminded him. "I vividly remember you saying that it was near the telecom tower."

"No," he repeated. "I never said that."

"Hang on a minute," I said. "Aren't you the man who called on Friday evening saying that you had land near the telecom tower?"

His answer startled me. "No, I have never called you."

"Then why did you get into my car when I stopped at the café?" I asked.

"Well, because I recognized the car. You are the man looking for land. I have land, and it is this way."

I couldn't believe my ears. I was totally annoyed. I wanted to turn back because someone else was waiting to show me his land near a telecom tower. The old guy protested. He said we would arrive at our destination in 15 more minutes.

I wasn't going to fall for that. I have learned over the years when the locals say "15 more minutes," it can really be another three hours or more.

"I have to go back," I said.

But the old man insisted. "Fifteen more minutes. If it is more than 15 minutes, then you can go back, I promise."

So I gave in. Indeed, to my surprise, after approximately 15 minutes, he told me to stop the car. We had arrived at his land. It was in the middle of nowhere. You couldn't really see a thing because it was hilly, with dense jungle all around. I didn't want to get out of the car. I wanted to go back to the coffee shop and meet the man who had called me. Yet, out of respect for my old passenger, I reluctantly disembarked. "I will take you to the highest point so that you can see," he said. We walked for about half an hour up hills and through valleys and eventually arrived at one of the highest points. I still couldn't see much so I climbed a tree. I went up a number of meters. As I looked over the site, my mouth dropped. I became breathless. It was the most spectacular site I had ever seen. Then I felt the words flow through me, "This is it. This is the site I want you to have so you can build the village." My eyes were filled with tears. I didn't know if I should shout with joy or cry.

"How many hectares do you want?" he asked. Well, I thought I wanted a minimum of 25 hectares, but how do you look at this sort of land filled with hills and valleys and know how big a hectare is? So in my excitement, I said that I would have all the land from the provincial road which we arrived on, to the logging road on the opposite side, and up until the river to the north, and the creek behind me to the south. I would have all that land. I had no idea how many hectares it was and how much it was going to cost, but that didn't matter to me because I didn't have a cent to my name anyway. I never told the man that. If he found out that I had no money to purchase the land, he would think I was crazy. I just knew if the Lord wanted us to have this land, then He was going to provide for it.

Weeks later I kept thinking about how the events of that day had unfolded. The man who called to say he had land near the telecom tower never contacted me again. It made me realize that this was obviously God's doing. He knew that I never would have gone to that remote area to look for land, so He had to come up with a scheme to get me to meet that old man to see his property. How clever was that. God works in mysterious ways at times. I am so grateful He got me there. We agreed to have the site surveyed so we could measure the dimensions. This mammoth task took about five months. Not only did we have to survey the land, but we also had to count the trees and contact their owners. You see, in the jungle, each tree is owned by a tribe or an individual, and to purchase the property, one also must purchase the trees. We learned that 15 different people owned the trees, while another 25 individuals and tribal groups owned the land. The man who showed me the site belonged to one of the local tribes, and he represented all the owners.

The survey determined that the land I chose totaled 111.6 hectares, or about 300 acres. Six months after our first visit to the property, we knew the size of the plot, the cost for each tree, and the price of the land. Remember, I told God the land had to be dirt cheap. We agreed to pay the equivalent of USD37,500, and it was now time for us to complete the transaction. Well, I had invested all my personal funds in the children's home in Sanggau, so I was broke. The deadline to seal the deal drew near and my local boys were becoming worried. They knew that if we didn't have the funds, our lives would be at stake. Literally, our heads could roll. As I had mentioned earlier, many people had lost their heads and lives in failing to keep a promise in a real estate transaction. My local team came to me, deeply concerned that I did not have the funds. But I assured them that God would provide. All we had to do was pray and believe. Then, just a week before the date set for signing the papers, money arrived in our missions account from various sources - families, churches, and individuals who knew nothing about our land purchase. But God knew. He provided through them miraculously so we could complete our deal on time. How awesome is that? Speaking of the size of our property, we have in the meantime added another 500 acres so now we have almost 800 acres, with plans to purchase another 200 acres. Those plans include the sites for our new hospital, another training centre, and our airstrip. God has miraculously provided funds each time we needed it!

We named the property Living Waters Village, not just because of the springs and river on the site, but because we constantly draw on God's river to sustain us in our multi-faceted mission of church planting, medical ministries, and caring for children and youth in crisis.

The Angry Mob

Soon after acquiring the property, a small group of local folks began helping me prepare a hut which became our first dwelling place on the land. One Sunday, we were getting ready to go to a nearby village to attend a worship service. A couple of visitors from New Zealand were our guests. When we looked out of our home, we noticed that we were about to be confronted by 40 or 50 angry locals bearing machetes and knives, heading directly toward us. I cried out, "Oh, Jesus, what shall we do?" I told our guests to quickly go out the back door, to walk or run, and start praying. The men in our house were instructed to start boiling lots of water.

I quickly opened the front door, not knowing really what I should do, to run or what. Without thinking, I found myself striding straight toward the mob with both arms outstretched. I said rather loudly, "Welcome everyone! What a lovely surprise! What gives us the pleasure of your visit today?"

Oh, you should have seen the look on their faces! They were puzzled and perplexed. They looked at each other as if to say, "What an idiot! Doesn't he realize we could lop his head off right now?"

I said, "Come inside and have some coffee with us. Please place your weapons outside and come on in."

Coffee was served but their angry faces didn't fade.

"Why are you here?" I asked.

"We are here because you are on some of our property," they explained, pointing out the disputed plot.

They demanded that we move off the site.

"No," I said. "This property is ours, and I have a registered certificate to prove it. Now if you also have a registered ownership certificate then we have a problem, but we will both then go to the police station and settle the matter. So where's your proof of ownership?"

"We don't have a certificate," they replied.

It turned out that the man who sold us the property was their uncle, and he had not approached them with regard to the sale. You see, in the jungle, a piece of property is owned by a tribe or family, and when it is sold, it is necessary to give part of the proceeds to each person involved. As the conversation continued, I said, "Look, I purchased the property from your uncle, and we did it in accordance with all of the laws of the land. You'll have to go to your uncle to settle this." The conversation now went on without tension and I offered them more coffee. They were ready to leave after making one request of us. "There are two small pieces of property adjacent to yours. Mister, if you decide to buy them, please come to us first." I assured them that we would contact them if we wanted to purchase their property. They left the house, picked up their weapons, and headed down the road. God had wonderfully protected us so we went off to church, ready to praise Him. I can tell you that my legs were like jelly when they left. I had the shakes all day after that, probably because of an overdose of adrenaline.

A few months prior to this event, some of our young men were confronted by a group of natives with machetes. They demanded that we immediately leave their property, and if we weren't gone when they came back, they would kill us all. Our young men ran inside and said that I should quickly go because they would be after me first. But I reminded them that it was God who brought us here, and no one was going to force or threaten us to leave. I told them to sit down because I could see they were afraid. Three months before we purchased our land, a group of locals had lopped off the heads of several people because of a land dispute, so my boys had every good reason to be afraid. But fear does not come from God. Fear comes from the enemy. The enemy loves to attack our faith by enticing us with fear so that our faith becomes stagnant and powerless. I sat down with my young men and we read Psalm 91 together. In that particular psalm, God had promised His divine protection.

I asked them, "Is this just a story or is this the Word of God?"

"The Word of God," they replied.

"Well then, believe it, and put it into practice. Go back to your tasks, and let this matter be settled by God."

More than a week later, the natives were back with their machetes, shouting that they were going to kill everyone - men, women and children. But this time one of my guys named Hengky stood up and shouted to them, "Okay then, you come now, but know this: there are more on our side waiting for you than there are on your side!" Now at this point, tremendous fear gripped the hearts of the natives because they did not know who was waiting for them. They were probably thinking that we had many tribal warriors lined up around the place armed with machetes. However, Hengky was referring to the angels of the Lord who were encamped around us and His chariots of fire. The words of faith spoken were more than enough for the enemy. They ran back into the jungle, and we never saw those men again. Praise the Lord!

It's Time to Build

The decision was made, the price was paid, and now we had 300 acres of jungle to develop. We didn't know where to start. This was a massive piece of property (I had even gotten lost twice in the jungle trying to figure out the layout of the land). For a brief moment, we were overwhelmed with the challenge before us. The property consisted of hills and valleys but no level spots where we could build. It made sense to first plan for roads and building sites. But I had never built a road or designed an underground utility network. When we moved onto the property, many of our boys who had already been with us for years took part in the planning process. Our vision became theirs. Some of our young men had just returned from Bible College. They were very excited about what God had entrusted to us. But most of them were wondering how this new vision was going to unfold. I invited them to walk with me to one of the highest points on the property. After quite a hike, we arrived.

Turning around, I asked them, "Tell me, what do you see?"

"Well, we see trees, lots of trees," they observed.

"Yes, okay, good!" I nodded. "Now, take another good look. Tell me, what do you see?"

They looked at one another, then took another look at the land. "Dad, all we see is trees, hills and valleys. Are we supposed to see something else? What do *you* see, Dad?"

"Boys, I see something very different. Over there, straight ahead of us, I see a huge training centre where many children will come fresh out of the jungle and live with us. They will learn how to live and care for each other, how to do away with their idols, and receive Jesus into their lives. Over there to the right, I see a large workshop where young people will be trained in vocational skills. That hill to our left will be leveled to create enough land for a school for 2,000 children. They will have the opportunity to be educated, from preschool to high school. Further to the left, I see a worship centre that will seat 2,400 people. They will learn to worship God, the Creator of heaven and earth, in spirit and truth. A bit further left, I see homes for 1,000 children, families, teachers and other staff. Where we are standing now I see a hospital where not only patients will be treated medically, but also where many nurses and doctors will be trained. Further to the right, I see an airstrip for a small aircraft to pick up and drop off patients from remote villages. That's some of what I see. Boys, we must be able to see what we cannot see. We must see this land with our spiritual eyes, not with our physical eyes. If we only see with our natural eyes, we will have a tendency to give up when the going gets tough, through exhaustion, disappointment, and discouragement. But when we see in the spirit the completed task that God has entrusted to us, even though we haven't even started yet, and even though it seems totally impossible to achieve in the natural, our faith will compel us to step out, start, and complete the task as we trust and obey Him in every aspect of our lives. Then we will see the impossible made possible, His miracles performed through His Holy Spirit who lives in us. Our faith and obedience will release all of His provision to complete the work, because what He starts, He finishes."

"So boys, have another look," I said. "Tell me, what do you see?"

"Yes, Dad, we see it. We see the training centre over there, the workshop on the other hill, the school on that side, the hospital and the buildings for the children, and the airstrip. Yes, we see it!"

"Really? That's strange. I only see trees and valleys," I joked.

When I told a number of my friends who are pastors and missionaries about my vision, they thought I had lost my mind.

"Build a home for 1,000 neglected children in the middle of the jungle? That's impossible!" they remarked. "How are you going to get your building materials to the site with such roads? Where's your money? You told us you were broke."

"I am," I said, "but God will provide."

"Where are your workers?"

"I don't know, but God will send them to us."

If I had listened to these people's reasoning, I probably never would have started. Yes, they were right. Logically it seemed impossible, it didn't make

Above: *Living Waters Village primary school.*
Below: *Some very happy Dayak tribal children. For many children and youngsters here in the jungles, there is no future without an education.*

Some of our enthusiastic Dayak tribal children enjoying school, something not available to many of them before coming to our village.

Thessa

sense. Yes, humanly speaking, it probably could not be done without having everything in place, but when God says do it, then we have two options – obey or disobey.

So we got started! I hired about 50 locals to come to the site with their machetes and axes. I gave them some guidelines for where to cut down trees and jungle growth, but the progress was extremely slow. After three months of work, the locals had only chopped about 300 yards of growth. The project was too big to be done with machetes. We had to find a faster way. "Oh, God, what shall I do? If we continue this way, it will take us years just to clear the road site."

Our property was situated on a logging road, and we frequently saw big trucks loaded with logs passing our front entrance. I reasoned, "Surely they must have some big bulldozers that they use in their operation. Maybe they will let us borrow one for a few weeks." So we drove for about two hours down the road to the headquarters of the logging company. Sure enough, many big machines were sitting there in their yards. We went to the office, introduced ourselves, and explained the reason for our visit.

"Gentlemen, we are the people who purchased the property up the road," I began. "It is a humanitarian project. We're going to build schools, a hospital, and homes for 1,000 children in crisis. The schools will accommodate the local children. Would you let us borrow one of your bulldozers to clear away a lot of jungle for our roads and building sites?"

“Sure!” they responded. “We’d be glad to help. Just give us an official letter explaining your plans, and we will provide you with a bulldozer.”

Two or three weeks later, a large earth-removing machine arrived at the entrance of our property. The machine operator stopped, turned off the engine, and just sat there. We walked over to the idle machine and asked the operator if he were coming in, but he said, “I’m waiting for paper work to arrive, sir.” After sitting there for a couple of hours, he got out from his machine, entered a waiting car, and disappeared.

We waited, but after a week, we decided to go to the logging company office to find out what was creating the delay. “Mister,” said the foreman, “we’ve just one request of you before we complete our agreement. When your hospital is built, we want you to provide free clinic and medical services for all of our workers and their families in your area.” Now this was a large operation employing hundreds and hundreds of workers. It was a request we knew we could not agree to. We graciously informed the man that we could not agree to such a request and left his office.

On the way back to the site we prayed for God to guide us to someone else who had the equipment we needed. In a few days, we were told about a Christian company in Pontianak that could help us. We made the 12-hour journey to the large seaport town to find the firm. We inquired about renting a bulldozer. It included the cost of a driver and transporting the machinery to our site. The prospect of maneuvering over poor road conditions drove up the price. For the transportation, fuel, operator, and rental of the machine, the bill added up to almost USD15,000 for one month.

We had USD15,000 in our account, but that was designated for food for the children, school fees, transportation, and other items related to the operation of the children's home. So we took a step of faith. We withdrew the money from our account and directed the firm to bring the bulldozer to our site and begin the work. We just believed that God would send in the funds by the end of the month so we could pay our bills. I had learned that when we seek to do God's will, we can take the first step of faith, and that opens the way for God to do His miracles. At the end of the month, the money needed appeared in our account again. Where did it come from? Some came from a church in Holland, some arrived from a couple in Belgium, and some came from a family in Australia. None of them knew we needed this money. But God did, of course.

Now, we had the bulldozer on our property and an operator ready to fire up its big diesel engine. What about the plans? How would we know where to carve roads and where to push away the jungle foliage? God was already at work. An Australian man had just finished a job at another mission station about ten hours away. He heard about our project and drove over to offer us assistance.

"What kind of work do you do?" I asked.

“I’m an electrician.”

“Well, we don’t have any electrical work at the moment. Maybe there’s something else you can do.”

“I’m a road builder.”

“Great! We’ve been praying for God to send us someone to help lay out the road system here on our 300 acres.”

“I can help. Just let me see your site plan.”

Of course, we didn’t have a proper plan, just a hand-drawn one. But a day or two later, a man from Holland arrived. He informed us that he had worked in Australia for 30 years on road projects. Fantastic! God had sent us two experienced men in road building, and now the operator of the bulldozer had some professional guidance. Amazing! Thank You, Jesus. What took 50 people with machetes and axes to do in three months, this mammoth bulldozer did in a few hours! What a thrill! In just one week, the site was transformed. Roads connected each building site, tying the property together in a city-like network.

Over the years, God has brought to us many people from around the world to help build a town in the middle of the jungle of Borneo. This phenomenal project is not our project but the Lord’s. Kay and I knew from the beginning that we could not do this on our own, and we had no desire to do so.

From the very beginning, we have said that our doors are always open for anyone who wants to experience what missions is all about. We want to provide people with that opportunity. People have been coming from all over the globe for a few weeks, a few months, and even a few years to help us fill the needed tasks. And so it has been a tremendous blessing to us to have so many professional and non-professional people come each year from various nations and different denominations. Teachers for our schools, medical staff for our clinic, administrators, builders, electricians, preachers, labourers, agriculturalists, plumbers, engineers, mechanics, musicians, worship leaders, singers, concrete workers, brick-layers, surveyors, cooks, painters, farmers, house-parents, cleaners, carpenters, dancers, artists, IT-people, architects, graphic designers, road builders, geologists, mums and dads, young people and children. God has sent them all. Everyone has God-given talents and gifts which they can use here. Those who come are a tremendous blessing to us. They also go home greatly blessed. Many express how God has changed them, powerfully challenged them, and inspired them while serving Him in our village. They go home with a different outlook on life. They realize that the Lord can use anybody if they are willing to make themselves available for whatever He has for them to do. People understand that even the little they have done for the Lord has often made a significant and lasting difference in their lives, and that gives such an incredible feeling of reward.

At the end of the month, we had to make another decision. We needed a grader, a compactor, and an excavator, but we were out of money. We told the firm in Pontianak of our need. They said, "We will send the equipment out immediately, and you needn't pay us until the end of the month." That was good news. We were out of money, but we were not out of faith. You see, faith is no license for foolishness, but we knew God was with us, and that our task was very important to Him. When those four massive machines went to work, the roads were soon completed, and the building sites were leveled.

The cost of hiring all those machines amounted to nearly USD50,000 for that month. But once again, at the end of the month the funds were in our account, and the bills were paid as agreed. Where did the money come from? "God" is the only answer I can give you. I don't know where most of the funds came from - various people and churches, no doubt. I just know that when it's God's project, and His servants remain faithful to Him, then His resources are unlimited.

A lot of people often ask me why we don't start up small business enterprises, like selling bread and cakes from our bakery. Some have suggested that we sell vegetables from our gardens, market our man-made concrete blocks, or tap our rubber trees. This could generate an income for the ministry so that we would not be so reliant on overseas funding. My answer is always the same. We are not now, nor will we ever be, reliant on overseas funding. We are totally reliant on the Lord for everything. Now, if He decides to use people from around the world to sponsor and support His work here, then that is totally up to Him. I understand though why He often does that. He uses people because it affects their faith as well. They learn to give, share, and understand the responsibility that God has given them concerning the plight of the world. But God can do anything. If He decides to drop a bag of money out of the sky on Living Waters Village, then I will be there to receive it. He just needs to tell me where He dropped it, so I can pick it up and use it. After all, He can do anything. This hasn't happened to me yet, but I'm ready when He decides to do that. I have seen a number of ministries which have started small enterprises. They often start off well; they are excited and depend on the Lord for everything, until one day they decide to start a small enterprise to generate some funds. The extra funds are great and certainly help. But they entice people to want more. More effort is then put into the business to produce more money, but before they know it, more and more time is taken away from the reason why they are there in the first place. We are here to evangelize, to disciple, and to care for the people. Their reason for being here has been jeopardized. It turns their ministry into a business organization rather than a center for evangelism and discipleship.

After three months, most of the work had been completed by the machines and they were returned to Pontianak. Next, we had to lay out the infrastructure for sewage, drainage, and electrical cabling underground. Because of the topography of the land, we determined that each building site would need its own septic tank. Because of our annual rainfall (between six and ten meters per year) the drainage system for the roads required concrete borders and drain ditches. All the concrete had to be mixed with small cement mixers and all the drain ditches had to be installed by manual labour. After nine years of work here on the site, only a few of the roads are complete since we cannot use asphalt for road covering. We use concrete which is far more permanent without having to hire expensive machinery.

At the time of this writing, we have constructed almost 60 buildings, with more than a hundred to go. We're building with the best materials available, but they have to be hauled on roads that are not really roads. I often say to overseas volunteers that in their country they have to go to a theme park and pay to ride roller coasters, but here, it is free every day. Just use our roads! We want the buildings to last until Jesus comes again, so they are constructed to the highest building codes and standards, and that's rare in our neck-of-the-woods. We make all of our own concrete blocks here on site, by hand. We employ many men from around the region. They can have a job with good wages to feed their families. We try and create as many jobs as we can so people don't have to live in poverty. Of course, this gives us a good report with the community at large.

It was time to build our training centre to house a few hundred children and young adults. This would be the nerve centre for the entire ministry. It was going to be a huge place and would require a lot of know-how and funds. A lot of people told us it couldn't be done because we just didn't have the expertise or the money. But that has never stopped me. God knew we needed this building to house all these kids whom nobody wanted. Hence, we just started and watched God perform the miracle. A number of people had come from various countries to help us. Allan from Australia helped design the building so we could follow the drawings. That was much easier said than done.

While I was shopping in Kuching for a number of days, a team of our young men was pouring the enormous slab of concrete for this big building. Weather conditions were just right. However, halfway through the day, an enormous storm suddenly appeared and approached the property from the south. Everyone knew that this was bad news. A downpour could destroy their day's work, not to mention all the concrete. One of the Western guys stood up, raised his hand to the storm, and said in a loud voice, "In Jesus' Name, rain, bypass this property." The rain sounded like an oncoming train. It did not bypass the property but miraculously bypassed the area where they were pouring concrete. Heavy rain drenched the left of the building site, but the area where the men were pouring concrete remained dry. The excavator driver and the bulldozer operator witnessed everything. Neither was a Christian. They were amazed. It was the subject of conversation for many days.

Weeks later, our team of young men was pouring concrete for the huge underground water tank at the training centre site. Again, a huge storm was approaching from the same direction. The sky darkened, and the rain approached like a huge wall. This time, a number of our men stood up, remembering what happened before. They believed that if God could answer the prayer of one man, He could respond to the prayers of many as well. They raised their hands to the storm and shouted, "In the Name of Jesus, rain, bypass this property!"

I was on a trip overseas at the time, but one of our young men described the scene later. "Dad, you should have seen it," he marveled. "We prayed, but the rain kept on coming. All of a sudden it hit the border of our property, and then, to the amazement of everyone, split in half. It poured to the left of us, and it poured to the right of us, but where we were pouring concrete, it was dry!"

Everyone stood there with their mouths open, just staring, including the bulldozer driver and excavator driver. Both were convinced now that there definitely was a God who loves and cares for His people. They both gave their lives to Jesus that week.

We baptized them in one of our creeks on the property. It was an incredible day of celebration for them and us, witnessed by many volunteers from

This was the first 111.6 hectares of land that we purchased miraculously. With its many hills and valleys it was relatively easy to get lost. This happened to me twice while I was trying to survey the land.

A few years later all the roads and building sites were leveled and cut out. It was a mammoth task. Buildings have been erected at a fast pace in order to accommodate the many children in crisis arriving each week.

Above: *A view of the original 111.6 hectares, plus on the left of the built-up area, another 180 hectares which we purchased over the years for an airstrip and hospital.*
Below: *In the beginning - our first hut on the property.*

around the world who had come that week to help out. After almost a year of hard work, the training centre was complete. What a joyous day that was! Many had called the building project impossible, but it was done, and it looked fabulous. What a wonderful gift from the Lord. We all moved in and had a thanksgiving service to rejoice in God's wonderful provision. I suggested early in the celebration that all of us simultaneously give the Lord a giant, jubilant shout of thanksgiving. Everyone wanted to join in, and after counting to three, we all raised our voices in unison to shout our appreciation to the Lord. At that very second, a strong wind suddenly blew into the building, startling us all. Although the wind came from a sudden storm brewing outside, we couldn't help believing that it was more than a coincidence. The evening worship and celebration were just awesome. God's presence felt so tangible many of us couldn't hold back tears.

An Army of Grasshoppers

Some years ago, our entire district came under attack from millions of huge grasshoppers that wiped out all the rice crops, vegetable gardens, and fruit trees. This terrible plague devastated thousands of people in a wide area. It obliterated their livelihoods and crops in just a few days. The local government had to step in to provide rice for the people. Many were starving. We heard about the disaster days after the attack. The news startled me because it happened all around us but not on our property. Our fruit trees and vegetable gardens were not affected. We were spared.

A few days later, I heard an eerily loud noise coming from a distance. To my horror, I saw an enormous dark mass approaching our property. It was the grasshoppers. I cried out loud, "Jesus, please send them away!" Then the miracle happened. They all landed on our roads but not on our gardens. In a few minutes, they flew away again, and that was the end of them. People living around us were astonished to learn that every garden and orchard in the district had been destroyed except those on our property. They wanted to know how this was possible.

One of our young men came back from a nearby town and noted, "Dad, do you know what people from other faiths are saying about us? They are saying to one another, 'Don't mess with those people on that land over there because their God is with them.'"

"Wow," I said, "are they really saying that? Good! Let them spread that news around a bit more. Don't mess with us because our God is with us. If you mess with us, you will be dealing with our God."

Utilities

One of the major challenges we faced when we started building was the matter of electrical service. Electricity poles from the government electric company did go right past our property. However, the cost to connect to them was astronomical, and we could only have electricity three nights a week. On top of that the supply was so erratic that it would go off several times a day. Besides this the voltage went up and down like a yo-yo and caused many problems for electrical appliances. Hence, we chose not to connect with the local electric company. Instead, we opted for our own generators. We started with a few smaller ones that would produce enough electricity for at least four hours a day from 5:30pm till 9:30pm. It gets dark here every day between 5:30pm to 6:00pm because we live on the equator. No change all year round. We only had power for four hours a day and were very limited where we could use it for. We couldn't have refrigerators, hot water boilers, toasters or anything like that. We basically had power for lights, battery chargers, and a fan here and there.

The generators were also so loud that they echoed throughout the valleys, scaring every creature away from our property. A lot of monkeys that used to raid our vegetable gardens and fruit trees stayed away when the generators were on. Now there are very few animals that visit our property. But the generator noise is not the only reason. Apparently, our kids just can't help themselves: They eat anything that breathes in the jungle. An animal is not a pet here, but food. I remember one day bringing back an animal picture book from Australia. Our children marveled at strange-looking creatures like the kangaroo, wombat, and cockatoo. They would ask, "Are they nice to eat?" or "What does that one taste like?" On another occasion, when we eventually had a television set, we were watching an Australian program about a veterinarian who treated sick animals. The first time our tribal children saw this, they were mystified. On the program, a lady brought in a bird that had broken its wing smashing into a windsreen.

The kids inquired, "What is she doing?"

"She is bringing the bird to the animal doctor because the bird has a broken wing," I explained.

They were stunned that there was such a person as an animal doctor.

"Why doesn't she just wring the bird's neck and eat the thing?" the kids asked.

I realized our worlds are so different. Who knows how many animals did not become meals because of our noisy generators?

Since our ministry was growing to include our school and children's homes, we needed far more electricity. Four hours a day would not be enough. We required much larger generators that could operate 24 hours a day. We started to pray and research to find out what would suit our needs. Eventually we came up with an 80 kva soundproof Caterpillar diesel-powered generator which would cost around USD25,000 each. The better ones were made in the UK, in Northern Ireland. Also, we found a distributor a 12-hour drive away from our place that could provide spare parts and services. God heard our prayer, and soon, the funds arrived! This time we knew where the money came from. A congregation in

England had just sold their beautiful church building that had served them well for years. When its members found out that we didn't have any electricity for our schools and children's homes, God laid it on their hearts to give a portion of the funds to our project. And indeed they did this. Praise God for their generosity! Those funds provided the cash to buy four large generators which have served our needs now for years.

There's another very vital need at the centre, and that is water. It rains frequently here, so we collect all the rain water from our roofs, and pipe it to huge underground concrete water storage tanks. We use this water for drinking. We have dammed the creek on our property, and from there, water gets piped to large PVC water tanks, then flows to various tanks at each building on our land. It is a huge network of water pipes. This water is for showers, toilets, cleaning, etc. It is a little complicated, but we have our own water system that serves our 600-plus residents in the children's home. We are self-sufficient with our electricity, sewer and water systems, which can all be expanded as our project grows.

One other enormous task is completing the miles-long road system. It will take tens of thousands of sacks of cement and miles of steel to finish. We must build concrete gutters on both sides of the roadway for drainage. With each tropical rainfall, a few more millimeters of road wash away. We receive six to ten meters of rain each year (about 20 to 33 feet). That's a lot, so we need to lay concrete before the roads slip down the hill. But I remember the promise God gave us: "I finish what I start." God can do anything!

The Hennesey Family

Our construction requires an endless amount of building material that is often difficult to obtain quickly. Hence, we must order many truckloads of goods, sometimes months in advance, to make sure enough stock is available to keep all our builders and labourers working. However, at the time we put in the order, there is usually no money. Goods are ordered in faith and when they arrive, they need to be paid up as soon as possible.

Two local businesses supply a lot of our building material. The owners of one of these local companies have even become good friends of ours. It is a real blessing that our main suppliers allow me enough flexibility with our credit so that an average of 40-50 truckloads of building material and food arrive each week at our ministry. However, I have set a credit ceiling of USD150,000, which I think is already a large amount. I have told the Lord that I don't want to ever pass that level.

I believe that we need much faith to build an entire town in the middle of the jungle, just as the Lord has asked us to do. But we cannot wait until we have 100 percent of the funds in hand to start the job, because if we did, then we wouldn't really need faith.

So we need to step out in faith, but I also believe that we require much wisdom. I don't believe that we should build this place on credit. To me, that is not faith. I believe that faith and wisdom often go hand in hand. Frequently, we hear of pastors who have started a huge building program. Some would even convince church members to mortgage their own homes so that their vision can be realized. However, when things start to go wrong, and the budget blows up to an unacceptable level, all of a sudden the pastor feels called by God to go somewhere else. The congregation is left with a giant debt that could take years or decades to pay. That is not wise. Faith has turned into foolishness.

And so I believe in paying bills on time and restricting the use of credit. It takes wisdom to maintain the right balance. I encountered this challenge a few years ago: each day I thanked the Lord for His incredible provision. I kept reminding Him that we were creeping up closer and closer to our credit ceiling, and that an extra boost of funding would be greatly appreciated. I determined that the following Tuesday was going to be the day that we would hit that limit. Without more funds, I would have to resort to drastic measures: all 80 of our builders and labourers would be sent home. Most of these guys had families to feed, and new jobs are hard to come by. If they did find another job, it would be difficult to get them back. So I didn't want to stop the building and send everyone home. Each day, I brought this problem before the Lord. On Tuesday morning, during my prayer time, I reminded the Lord of the deadline. If no extra gifts came in that day, then I would have to start winding things down, something I dreaded. In my prayer, I told the Lord I believed that He could do anything. Nothing is impossible for Him. So again I thanked Him for taking care of the problem. If He chose not to do anything extra, then of course I would accept it, but if He could then please give me the wisdom to know what to do next.

I asked the Lord to remind Mr. Hennesey from England that we were still here in Borneo. Four years earlier, he had surprised us with a wonderful gift of USD120,000. It went a long way furthering our ministry. But we had not heard from him since that generous contribution.

Later that afternoon, I sat down with coffee and opened my emails. One of the first emails was from World Outreach UK, informing me that this morning a cheque arrived in the mail for us from Mr. Hennesey, worth almost USD450,000. Needless to say, my eyes nearly popped out of their sockets! I burst out crying, and praised the Lord with shouts of thanks and joy. I hadn't heard from Mr. Hennesey for four years and I mentioned him in my prayers only that morning. Of course, Mr. Hennesey had already sent that cheque in the mail a few days earlier, but what a miracle – so timely and such an incredible blessing. We were able to pay all that we owed and stock up on many more building supplies.

The training centre in progress – the building that many declared impossible to build. But God's ways are different from our ways. What seems impossible for us is certainly possible for Him.

Almost finished.

The current view of a section of our village from one of the water towers.

Tribal Culture Head On

Missionary life is very difficult and challenging. But frequently, situations and events occur that bring us moments of laughter and joy. For example, take the adjustment to a new culture. In most cases, when we do something that is against social or personal procedure, the tribal people are gracious and forgiving. One thing we learned is that the natives tend to be very generous. They will give you all they have, which is extremely limited because of their poverty. Because we do not wish to offend them, we accept whatever they offer. Sometimes, especially when it comes to food, this stretches our kindness to the limit. It isn't always that simple.

Let me explain. In my early months on the mission field, I was told that when dining with the locals, we must eat everything and leave nothing. On one occasion, some of our young men and I were visiting a village and accepted a dinner invitation. We sat down to eat with the man of the house. The wife and children didn't join us, but did serve the meal. I noticed that this poor family had purchased some eggs, which are very expensive in our area. So with great joy and pride, our hosts set the eggs in the middle of the table along with the other food.

Now, in order not to offend, I made sure everything was eaten, including all the eggs. After dinner, the family graciously bid us goodbye, and we went on our way.

In the car, one of my local boys confronted me, "Dad, don't ever do that again!"

"Do what?" I asked.

"Eat all the food! You must always leave some food for the wife and the children after we leave. You ate everything on the table!"

"But I didn't want to offend them!"

I felt terrible. I just ate the kids' food. And that day I learned to ask questions about the cultural expectations before proceeding.

The Jungle Toilet

A few years ago, four or five of our native church planters joined me on a visit to a tribe that lives in a longhouse. About 20 or 30 families reside together, each with its own sleeping areas, but most of the living is done in a communal setting. They cook their food and even share their evenings together in conversation. It is a wonderful environment if everybody gets along. These longhouses, built on poles, are usually located next to rivers. Animals live beneath the houses. The poles are made of an extremely hard wood called "ironwood," and the floor is raised six to 12 feet above the ground. The length of longhouses varies, depending on the number of families living together. When one arrives, a meal is prepared, and one is expected to eat with them.

After the meal, on this particular visit, I

urgently needed to use the toilet. Turning to the chief, I asked where it was.

"Go through that door which takes you outside of the building," he directed.

"Well, is the toilet to the right or to the left as you go out?" I inquired.

"Oh no, you just go outside anywhere," he said. "Do you have to do a number one or a number two?"

"I am not going to tell you," I replied. That's private information.

He said, "I just want to warn you. If you want to do a number two, you must take a stick with you."

"Why do I need a stick?" I wondered.

He explained that the pigs in the jungle can be very impatient. They don't always wait until you are finished, so you need a stick to hit them and keep them away from you until you are done. Otherwise you could experience a very unpleasant surprise. My imagination went wild. (Needless to say, I made sure I always had a stick on hand after this.)

Excusing myself, I headed for the door. I walked into the jungle for a bit and found a spot to squat. There I was with my stick, minding my own business, when all of a sudden I heard something behind me. I thought, "Wow, already there is a pig coming. Boy, they are quick, but praise God, I have my stick, and I am ready for any pig." As I slowly turned to hit the pig over the head, I was startled. It wasn't a pig. Peering out of the leaves of the jungle were these big brown eyes of several children who wanted to witness the event. I yelled at them to leave, but they stayed, their eyes riveted on my backside.

"What do you want?" I asked.

One of the older boys replied, "Mr. White Man, we are thinking this: our skin is chocolate color, and our number two is chocolate color, too. But you are White Man with white skin, and we want to see if your number two is white as well."

"No, mine's not white," I assured them. "It's chocolate color, same as yours. Now go away and let me finish."

They disappeared into the jungle, and I finished my task. Come to think of it, their inquisitive mind was not far off-centre.

Village Delicacies

On another tribal visit, it came time to join the people for the meal they had prepared. They were very poor, yet so honored that we were there. As their guest, I was asked to serve myself first. I took a small serving of rice, and on the rice I put a few scoops of soupy stuff they had made. It consisted of some green long vegetable things they found in the jungle and other things that were all foreign to me. I took a couple of small pieces of meat in the juice, and placed them over the rice. Mixing whatever looks questionable with the rice is often the best way to get it down.

As I was eating the first piece of meat, I was wondering what it actually was. It had lots of little bones but little meat. It wasn't delicious, but it wasn't disgusting either. It was just edible. And so I finished the first little portion of meat with a larger portion of rice, and now it was time to start on the second piece of meat. Taking my spoon, I touched the second bit of meat and as I did, it rolled over on my plate. To my horror, I realized that I had been eating a rat. The second bit of meat was the head of a rat with its teeth in its snout and its eyes still in its socket. It was as if the rat was staring at me. I stared at the rat, wanting to scream. I remembered thinking to myself, "Stay controlled, don't screw up your face in horror, as the people will be offended and won't want to listen to our Gospel presentation." I looked at the lady who cooked the meal. She smiled at me; I smiled back as if there was nothing wrong. But inside me, World War Three was about to break out. Everything inside me revolted at the thought of eating rat meat, and everything I had already eaten suddenly came back in my throat ready to be vomited. "Oh God," I cried within me, "please help me to forget what I have just seen, otherwise I am afraid I will throw up and offend everyone here." I started to think of beautiful trees, colorful flowers, and my wife eating spaghetti at home, and all sorts of other things to try and forget what I had just eaten and what was still on my plate. Gently and courageously, I pushed and pulled the head apart and moved it to the edge of the plate as if I had already tried eating it. I consumed the rest of the rice and vegetables. Praise the Lord, it all stayed down. It's amazing how the power of the mind can take over in situations like that. God was so gracious in helping me.

Soon we were excused from the table, and I relaxed. But I learned that day that saying grace before eating takes on a whole new meaning here in the jungle. Christians living in developed nations say grace very differently from missionaries on the mission field. People often say grace quickly. They want to get started with their meal, so the words that are prayed are often said without much thought or meaning. But here on the mission field, our prayer over our meal is a very serious matter. "Oh, God, have mercy on us, as we are about to eat this food without knowing what it is. Please BLESS it and if there is anything still alive on my plate, kill it now in Jesus' Name." We pray this prayer with intense fervor, but still we get sick at times. I've spent a few times in the hospital, deathly sick with food poisoning from eating food in the jungle

The Floating Floaties

Another time, we tried to reach the Red Feet Tribe, whose entire life is spent living in the trees. They believe that when their feet touch the ground they will be cursed. But as the day wore on, we knew that we couldn't get to the tribe, so we accepted the invitation of another tribe living along the river to spend the night in its village. One of the traditions is the communal bath. Our host asked us to go down to the river for a refreshing bath before supper. Grabbing our soap and shampoo, we joined the chief down at the riverside.

Floating in the river were all these little huts on pieces of logs, tied with ropes to the trees to keep them from slipping away. These little one-meter square huts made of palm leaves and bamboo served as individual toilets for the village people. There must have been at least two dozen huts, all tied to the trees along the water's edge. It was quite convenient as everything just plopped into the water and the current would just simply carry it away. However, this was also the place where people were brushing their teeth and washing their dishes and clothes.

When we got to the edge of the river and saw all these "floaties" floating by, I called out to the chief and asked, "Is this where we're going to take a bath?"

"Oh, yes!" He waved at me, "It's very refreshing!"

I thought, "Great, God, that's all I need, having a poo bath."

But then again, who knows what it will do for our complexion? All these floaties, rich in vitamins and minerals, may do us some good. I told one of my young guys traveling with me to go upstream a bit and let me know when there is a break in these floaties floating by, so that we could have this communal bath without offending anyone.

Some of our girls at the training centre.

Above: *Kuriok and her little brother. They are from the Matee tribe.*

Above: *Pener and grandchild from the Matee tribe.*
Bottom: *A delicacy dish of finger-licking bat stew that the local people love. In fact, anything that breathes, flies, crawls, or moves in any way is a delicacy to them. Our children caught these bats quickly and threw them straight into the wok without gutting or cleaning them. A little salt, pepper, and garlic, and all the children were staring at the brewed stew with mouthwatering excitement, hardly able to wait for this unexpected feast.*

Climbing down the river embankment to board a canoe. It takes us to the next village on the river to bring the Gospel message.

On the Melawi River on our way to the next village with the Good News.

A maze of waterways are the transport roads in the interior of Borneo.

Shortly after, he yelled out, "I would go in now if I were you."

So without hesitation, we all jumped in with our shampoo and soap. We probably had the quickest bath ever. I think I stunk more when I got out of the river than when I went in, but it really didn't matter because we all smelled the same, so no big deal. The worst thing was when this little old lady came toward the river with a small pail. She filled it, and left for her hut to prepare a nice cup of tea for us.

The Real Hot-Dog

On a different occasion, we were visiting one of our church planters. His home was located in the rural area, not in the dense jungle. A road passed in front of the home, and the traffic was minimal. That day, we received an invitation to share a meal with him and his family. As we ate, I noticed that our host was restrained in his conversation.

Finally, he said, "I'm really sad today."

"Why, what's wrong?" I asked.

"Our dog died this morning," he revealed.

"Ah, your dog?" I said.

I thought to myself, good for the dog. Most dogs in our area suffer from skin diseases, worms, and malnutrition. His dog was no exception. In fact, it always looked really sick. To me, his dog was better off dead than alive. That was certainly kinder to the animal. So I expressed my regrets and asked him what happened.

"He was hit on the road by a truck."

To keep the conversation going, I asked where the dog was buried.

"Oh," he said, "we didn't bury him. We just scraped him off the road, cooked him, and that is what you are eating now."

Well, this time I did scream out in horror. I just ate some of his sick dog! I couldn't eat anything anymore. All the food I had swallowed sat in my throat ready to burst out. I had a difficult time keeping it under control. One of the toughest assignments in missionary work is to eat the locals' food with grace and control. That is why you never ask what is being served before you eat. It is better not to know. Here is where faith takes over, and you proceed without showing fear or dislike for the taste. It is often *after* you have eaten when the surprise comes.

The Longhouse Toilet Nightmare

The most embarrassing moment I have ever experienced was not long after I arrived on the field. We were in one of the Iban tribe longhouses, sitting on the wooden floor in the communal area sharing the Gospel with the tribal chief and a number of tribal leaders. Because I was still getting used to all the exotic food, my stomach was upset; I'd already had diarrhea for a few days. While talking to these leaders, I really had to go to the toilet, but I did not want to interrupt the conversation. I thought I could hold it in for a little longer. But all of a sudden, my stomach revolted, and I knew if I didn't go immediately, then all hell would break loose. So I quickly asked the chief for directions to the toilet, hoping he would say it was outside. Instead he said, "Right there." He pointed to the kitchen, three meters away (almost ten feet). The kitchen was a two-by-two meter (nearly seven-by-seven foot) room where a few women were seated on the wooden floor, chopping vegetables. Right next to them, only a meter away (about a yard), was the entrance to the toilet. It had a toilet door which was open on the bottom and on the top there was a gap of about 30 cm (just less than a foot). The ladies could see directly into the toilet. I had no time to think of another solution, for I was about to explode. I opened the toilet door which had a loud squeak, and as I entered this little box, I realized to my horror there was no toilet paper! People here use their left hand to wipe their backsides, but I had no time to really consider an alternative. I looked down. The toilet was a hole in the floor boards. It was not a big hole, but who cares at such a moment? I was about to explode if I didn't hurry. I had to watch out where to put my feet: all around the hole, the boards were as rotted as anything because people had been missing the mark over the years. The house was on high stilts, and I didn't want to plunge through the rotten floor boards. On top of all this, my head got caught in a thick layer of cobwebs which were never disturbed because the local people were so short. I hate spiders, but I had really no time to contemplate that. To top it all off, all of a sudden I noticed a lot of noise under the house. As I looked through the hole, I could see pigs that had gathered around the bottom. They heard the toilet door open, and to them that meant it was time for dinner. I tell you, so many things were going through my head. "How, oh my God, am I going to go to the toilet with these women just a meter away chopping vegetables on the floor with a complete view of all that is going on? The tribal leaders are three meters away, the pigs are waiting for a good meal under the house, and there is no toilet paper to clean up!"

I thought to myself, "I will aim well and try and go very quietly. Perhaps the people will not notice." Well, my intentions were good, but oh boy, all of a sudden there was this massive explosion that rocked the toilet and rattled the door, with a smell that gassed every living thing in the vicinity. Even the pigs disappeared. But the most embarrassing thing was that nothing ended up in the hole. It sprayed everywhere despite my strategy. What a horrible mess. I had to creatively dispose of the matter. As I emerged from the toilet, I noticed that everyone had vanished. The women were gone. The tribal leaders were gone. In fact, there was nobody around anywhere. "Hello, hello, is anybody there?" I called out, but the whole place was deserted. I couldn't blame them. I wanted to crawl home and never come back again. I think I was the talk of that village for a long time.

Crocodiles

While visiting a number of villages on the river network, we came to a halfway point and spent the night in one village. It was so humid and hot, we all took a dip in the river. Before we went in, I asked one of the local leaders if there were any crocodiles in the river. He said, "No, no. No crocodiles here." The water looked really dirty from sand that washes into the river after a heavy rain. That occurs almost every day, making the water a murky reddish brown. If there was a crocodile or snake, you would not be able to see it at all. We enjoyed our half hour wash and swim. As we waded out of the river, I heard two locals talking about one of their tribal men. A crocodile attacked him the week before. He lost a big chunk of his thigh. He survived but was in a terrible mess.

"How terrible!" I exclaimed. "Where did this happen?"

They pointed, "On the other side of that hill over there."

"Is there another river system over on the other side?" I asked.

They answered, "No, it is the same river as this one."

"But you just told me that there are no crocodiles in this river."

"They are not here but around the corner over there."

Well, I nearly fell over backwards. We could have been lunch for the crocodiles. Since then I phrase my questions differently, "Are there any crocodiles at all anywhere in this entire river, left and right?" I just want to be sure.

De-worming Tablets

In one village, we brought de-worming tablets for there were many people who were riddled with worms. When I offered the tablets, everyone refused. They kept saying they didn't want worms. They thought the tablets would *give* them worms. It didn't matter how much I tried to convince them that the tablets were meant to *get rid* of worms. They weren't interested. After several attempts to explain, I gave up. Two weeks later, I came back with a new approach. I asked who would like some "special vitamins." Suddenly, everyone wanted them because they knew vitamins are good for them. And so, they received their "special vitamin," not realizing that they were really de-worming tablets. Where there is a will, there is a way.

Our state road, which is the artery for all vehicle transport. Needless to say, it's an enormous challenge when we go shopping, not knowing how long the journey will really take.

One of the many potholes on the Borneo highway during the rainy season.

A massive jungle bridge

Toher, Ronny, Yono, Hengky, Sujiman and Yanto checking out the border of our property.

Harvest time in the neighbourhood. However, what we really need is a great spiritual harvest in the white and ripe fields.

One of our vegetable gardens growing some wonderful produce.

The Vision on the Hill

A couple of years ago, I went through a deep spiritual valley. Everything seemed to be going wrong. The government had changed many of its regulations, and we were under pressure to comply. The tribes in our area were threatening us, and we had no idea how to appease them. Many of the children were undergoing major challenges. They had difficulty getting used to our rules and regulations. Before they arrived at our place, they could do whatever they wanted, like smoke, drink alcohol, and have sex with whomever they wanted. But now they couldn't. There was also much unrest among our missionary families. Other pressures were taking their toll on me. I was ready to quit and walk away from it all. I was in my third week of a 40-day fast, seeking the Lord for a breakthrough. I did not eat a thing, yet still worked at the same pace. As a result, my body was weak and my spirit depressed. Satan was all-out with his attack, and it seemed like I was beginning to fold.

While all the children were having lunch, I decided to walk and pray. I headed toward the hill we had leveled for our praise and worship centre. I just wanted to be alone with God. Near the top of the hill, I suddenly heard a voice saying, "Ronny, here, I am going to gather the tribes together." As I turned around to see who was speaking, all of a sudden a clear picture appeared in front of me, like someone just dropped me in front of a cinema, blocking out my normal vision. I saw thousands and thousands of tribal children and youth standing on this hill with their arms raised straight up to heaven, crying out intensely to the Lord. I just stood there completely paralyzed and stunned. I shook like a leaf and burst out crying. A voice within me said, "Ronny, what I start, I finish. Do not quit. Do not allow the pressures of this world to fog up your vision. Do not allow the building program, or the problems that people cause get in the way of what's important. Remain focused. This, what you see now, is what it's all about." God knew that I was so close to quitting. He was encouraging me to keep going and stay focused on what was important. The tribal people so desperately need Jesus in their lives.

The walk back to the training centre was easy. My heart was light, and the pressures seemed to have all vanished. When I arrived back at the office I shared my experience with some of the staff. A number of them wept and rejoiced. The next day was a wonderful day. My spirit was full of joy; the depression melted away. In addition, the problem with the tribal people had been resolved, the government officials retracted their demands, and the children seemed to be at peace.

Joy's Challenge

God's timing is always perfect. I remember a time when we went to Kuching to do our monthly shopping, collect our mail and have our car serviced.

After four days of shopping, we were ready to go back home. Our car was completely full. There were more goods on top of the car than in the car. We always get a lot of looks from people when we drive by because our roof-rack is packed high and wide. We got through the border without any hassles, but an hour later, the car started to stall. I noticed steam coming out from under the hood. The radiator hose burst, the engine overheated, and the engine-head was wrecked. I ended up chartering a van to transport Kay, the kids, and all purchases to our home. I towed the car back over the border to the closest mechanic in Kuching since there was no place in Kalimantan where our 4-wheel drive could be repaired. The mechanic reported repairs would cost USD2,000. We had no money; we had just spent it all on our shopping. I asked the mechanic how long it would take to repair the car. He said it would take five days. In faith, I told him to start, and I would be there in five days to pay and pick up my car.

I headed to the home of our friends, Mervyn and Edna Song. We normally stay with them when in Kuching. I prayed, "God, You know our ministry can't do without our car, so thank You that You will make it possible to pay the bill in five days' time." When I arrived at our friends' place, I received a call from Kay, who had safely arrived home. She informed me that World Outreach Australia had just phoned to let us know it had just received a cheque from a lady named Joy in Townsville. The amount - AUD2,500 - which at the time was about USD2,000!

Wow, how amazing is that! World Outreach asked if we needed the money quickly. Of course, I replied. It was exactly the amount we needed for the car repairs. What a fantastic answer to prayer. Thank You, Jesus!

I decided to write this lady to thank her for her timely and accurate gift. A few weeks later, I received her response. She confessed she almost did not send us the money. Apparently, she had sold her property and she was told by the Lord to give a portion of it away. She felt the Lord prompting her to give it to us, the Heyboers in Borneo. But she put the idea on the shelf for a while and kept on forgetting to send it. She also had difficulty finding someone who would help pass on the money to us.

Finally the Lord firmly reminded her again and eventually she managed to send it to us. When she received my letter thanking her for saving our day, she said she cried because she nearly didn't send it. She nearly disobeyed God. She almost got in the way of God performing a miracle for us. He could have and perhaps would have called someone else if she hadn't obeyed, but He called her to act and respond to His prompting. Praise God, she listened. Through her obedience we were blessed, our car was repaired, and I was able to go home again and be with my beautiful extended family and continue God's work.

Metje Hoffman

Our daughter Tanja visited us for a few weeks. During this period we were travelling by car doing some ministry work when a motorbike passed us. It swerved all over the place. The driver and passenger looked like some teenagers who were having fun, but not realizing they were endangering themselves and others. They slowed down and I passed them but the reckless driver raced ahead again. Annoyed at this dangerous game, I passed the motorbike again, and motioned for it to slow down or stop. Unfortunately, I cut them off slightly. I stopped the car and got out to talk with them. They stopped as well. When they removed their helmets, it was clear they were not teenagers at all. They were local adults who were short and very drunk. They came over and beat me up. They aimed for my head; I covered it with my arms. Car traffic stopped in both directions. I cried for help, but nobody came to my aid. It seemed everyone was afraid. Our 3-year-old Nathaniel screamed loudly in the car seeing his dad being beaten up. Both Kay and our 13-year-old son Paul dashed out of the car to help, but got hit over the head. Finally a plain-clothed policeman came running up the road waving his police badge. The attackers immediately retreated, but they kept on shouting abusive words that didn't make much sense because the men were so intoxicated. The officer requested I come to the local police station to file a criminal report so the men could be charged. I declined. I simply wanted to get my family home safely and forget about the whole incident. The police officer said he would lock up the two drunken men and let them sleep it off. Arriving home, we tended to our

Baptizing a number of our youngsters in the river on our property, in the Name of the Father, the Son and the Holy Spirit.

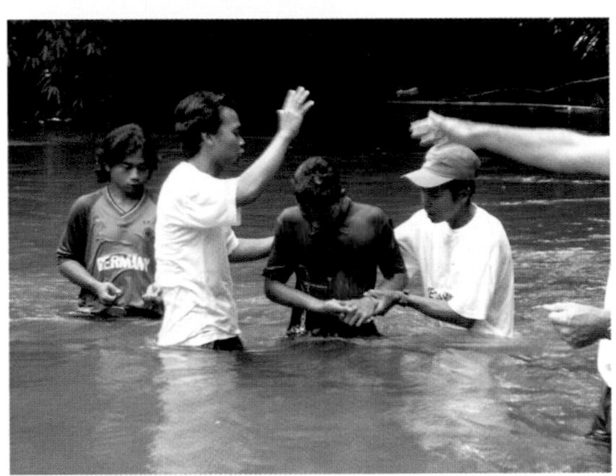

Worshipping the Lord our God with everything they have, in Spirit and in Truth.

Each day our children and students enjoy Bible readings and studies. They learn how to apply them to their daily lives. It is wonderful to see a new generation hungry for the things of God. The Scriptures transform their thinking; they become new people in Christ. We provide a personal Bible for each young person, thanks in part to our generous financial supporters.

bruises. Some members of the church came over to comfort us. They were very upset. "You should never stop for anyone in this part of the world," they said. "People can be dangerous here."

In the evening, our children asked me, "Why did God allow this to happen? Why didn't He protect us?" I told them of a testimony shared by a good friend of mine, Metje Hoffman. The lovely Dutch lady had lived decades in Australia. Her husband had died many years before. I used to visit Metje frequently, as part of our church's pastoral care for the elderly. Because of our shared Dutch culture, we talked and enjoyed fellowship many hours together and became good friends. During one of my visits, she excitedly told me that she was going to Brisbane to see her family. Metje hadn't seen her children in years and couldn't wait to meet them and her grandchildren. After she had been in Brisbane for a week, we got news that she was hospitalized after a robbery. When my elderly friend arrived back in Townsville, she shared her story with me. She had decided to go shopping in the city. While she was walking along the footpath, two young men grabbed her bag. She tripped and slammed her face on the concrete path. She was hospitalized with extensive bruises and cuts to her face and body. It was extremely painful.

Each day, she repeatedly asked God, "Why did You allow this to happen? I pray to You every day, thanking You for everything and asking You for protection for my family, friends and myself. All these years, You have looked after me so well. Why did You now fail me? What happened? Where were You? Why, oh why, did You allow this? I don't understand." She said that after a few days, a voice as clear as anything said to her, "Who else will pray for those two robbers?" She was shocked about this revelation. But she let the words sink in. She understood she was the one to pray for those two youngsters. They obviously didn't know God yet. They probably came from a broken home and never had anyone care for them, let alone pray for them. How would they come to know God? She said, "Ronny, ever since God revealed this to me, I have been praying for those two men. I don't know their names, but God does, and He cares for them as much as He cares for me. I will pray for them every day while I still have air to breathe, bringing them before the throne of God, asking Him to reveal Himself to those two young men. I pray that they, too, will have an opportunity to embrace Jesus Christ as their Saviour. If I had to suffer a little in the hospital, so what? Jesus suffered much more for me. I have been given the task to pray for them. I know that one day I am going to meet those two men in heaven."

And so I told my children that evening, "Who else is going to pray for those two drunken men we met today? They, too, obviously don't know God yet. We don't know their names either, but God does, and He cares for them as much as He cares for us. Let's bring them each day before the throne of God, asking Him to reveal Himself to them so that they can meet

Jesus our Saviour Who wants to be their Saviour as well." We all agreed and prayed for them for a long time.

Handono

Several years ago, one of our workers asked us to pray for his younger brother, Handono, who was 13 years old. He lived in a village named Pana, which belongs to the Pangkodan tribe. He accidentally drank something similar to battery acid from a bottle, thinking it was water. As a result of this his esophagus was burned and fused shut. Handono could not swallow food or water. It was even difficult for him to breathe, which meant his brain wasn't receiving enough oxygen. His words were difficult to understand, and his thoughts were tangled and incoherent. His parents, who loved him, took him to every witchdoctor they could find. They sold their land and goods and spent all their money looking for a cure, but no one could heal him. Finally, they took him to the nearest hospital and left him there for treatment. However, the local hospital had limited medical equipment and no doctors who could treat such a serious trauma. They inserted a small feeding tube through a hole they made in his stomach, but he developed an infection, and they pulled it out again. Other attempts failed and eventually, they left him there to die.

All of us prayed for Handono for three days, from Friday to Sunday. Finally on Monday, I told Kay, "I cannot just pray for him. I must go see him and find out if there is anything we can do." I was compelled to see the lad. I took a few of our young guys with me and drove five hours down the road to the hospital. He was severely dehydrated, riddled with scabies, and lying on a disgusting blood-stained mattress. It wasn't his blood; it was blood from several previous patients. The local doctors had given up on him, and he was just lying there waiting to die.

I sent one of our young men to the Immigration Department to get a passport for Handono. We decided to take him to Malaysia for treatment. The hospitals there are much better equipped. Normally, it can take up to two weeks to get a passport, but we couldn't wait that long. Our patient was dying. We all prayed for a miracle. When the officers learned of our emergency request, they issued the passport within hours. Carefully, we placed Handono in a van with a mattress, and journeyed on a bumpy road to the border. At the border, we transferred him to another van and drove slowly to the city of Kuching. We arrived at the general hospital late in the evening. Doctors examined Handono and referred us to another hospital in town. At the second hospital, the physician looked at Handono's throat and body. "Sir," he concluded, "I believe I can help, but his treatment will be complicated. We'll carefully peel open the esophagus to insert a tiny feeding tube for much-needed liquids and food. In the next few days, I will do several procedures to enlarge the feeding tube as long as his tissue does not tear. Once his body gains strength from the nutrients, we'll conduct a major operation. We'll take a portion of his intestine to form a new esophagus. Now, I've never done this before on children, but if you'll give us permission, we will start. And, sir, this will be an expensive procedure."

It would cost several thousand dollars, and I didn't have the money. Yet in faith we advised him to proceed, and God provided. The progress was slow but encouraging. After six weeks, Handono looked like a totally different person. A huge transformation had taken place. His body had gained so much strength, and he was now ready for surgery. All of us at the children's home prayed and rejoiced, knowing that God was on our side. The operation was a success. After a few more weeks, God had completely healed his body, thanks to the wonderful doctors and nurses in Kuching. When Handono arrived at the children's village after his operation, he couldn't talk much, and what he said was often erratic and didn't make much sense at all. Then one day, about a month after his arrival, we were sitting together, watching the children at play. Suddenly, he looked up at me and said, "Bapak, when I grow up, I want to be a doctor so that I can help people like the doctor who helped me." God had just done a miracle in restoring his speech and mind! We hugged each other in joy. He had not spoken like that since the day he accidentally drank the poison. Now his speech was clear, and his mind normal. People from different countries had donated funds to pay for the

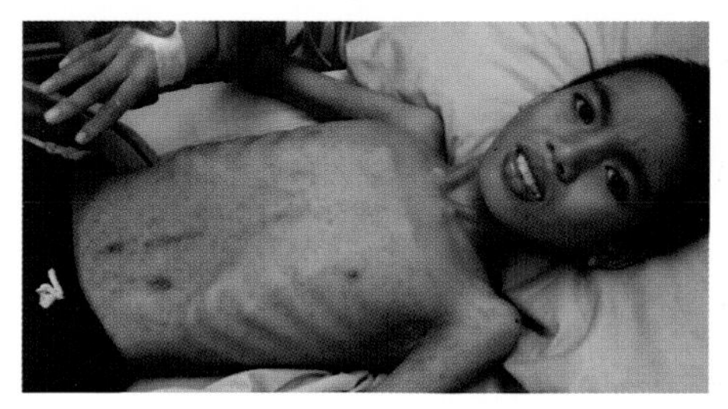 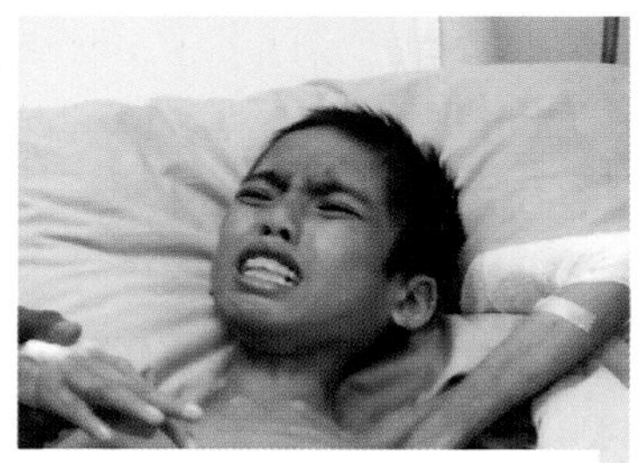

Handono when we found him left for dead because no one knew what to do with him. He could hardly breathe, and could not eat or drink. He accidentally swallowed something like battery acid, thinking it was water.

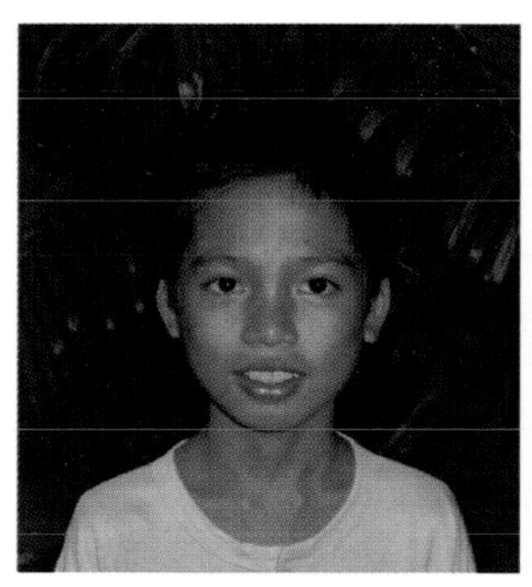 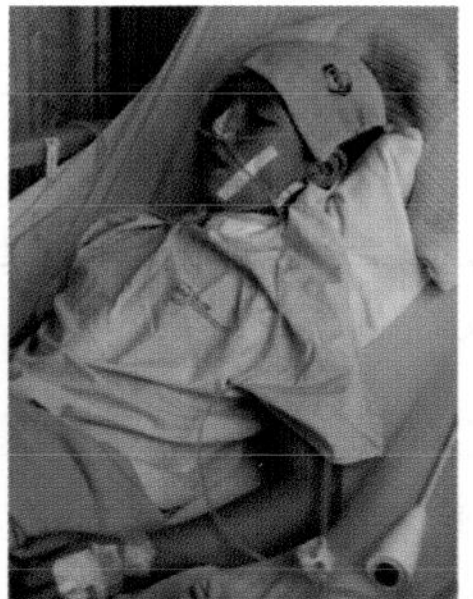 

Left: *Handono 6 weeks after we found him, after a number of small throat operations, getting ready for a major surgery to replace a section of his esophagus with some of his intestine.*
Middle: *Handono recovering from major surgery.*
Right: *Handono now in his senior year of high school, completely healed, loving God, and passionate in sharing with people about our awesome, great, and powerful God.*

operations and treatment. What an awesome God we serve!

Now I want you to catch the vision with me. When our hospital is built, cases like Handono's can be addressed right here on our site. With our airstrip operational, we can fly in doctors and surgeons from nearby cities. We are only an hour's flight away from Kuching, with another couple of hours to Singapore. Doctors can treat patients at our site and then return home at the end of the day. This is my prayer and dream, and I believe it is also God's. Just maybe in the years to come, Handono may be a surgeon at our new hospital.

We already have a medical centre, ready to serve the area, but its services are limited. We have a dental clinic, and dentists from Belgium, New Zealand, Australia and other countries come in for a few days, weeks, or months each year to serve the needs of our children.

At the time of this writing, Handono is 17 years old. He is doing wonderfully in his studies, and is a great blessing to us here at the children's home. He will make a great leader. Last year when I was preparing some photos for a ministry trip, Handono walked in and saw the pictures, "Oh my goodness, that kid looks terrible. Who is that?" I told him that it was him, when we first got him. He didn't even know. I realized then that I had never told him all the details of his miracle. After hearing the whole story for the first time, he had tears in his eyes. Now he is sharing his testimony in churches, telling people to trust in God, for He is able to do anything. If God can do a miracle for him, God can do a miracle for anyone. Just keep believing.

Interceding in Obedience

One morning, I received an email from a lady in Sydney, Australia, asking me what on earth had happened. She was awakened by the Lord the night before. He prompted her to pray and intercede for the Heyboers in Borneo. She immediately obeyed, not knowing what to pray for specifically. The urgency to pray became intense; she sensed that we were in danger. She said she prayed and wept for hours and then felt a breakthrough. She tried to go back to sleep but couldn't. She then emailed, asking us what had occurred. What danger were we in? As I read the email, I was a bit surprised. There wasn't any danger, and I wasn't aware of any impending danger. I immediately wrote back. I thanked her for obeying the promptings of the Lord to urgently pray for us. I told her that nothing disastrous was going on, but who knows what calamity her obedience prevented.

That morning, two of our older girls, Ana and Yolanda, went together to the market to buy vegetables and meat for the day. They rode a small boat to cross the intersection of the Kapuas and Melawi Rivers. On their way back after a successful shopping trip, they were about to step onto the dock, when a guy stood up in another boat, shouted, and aimed his gun straight at Ana. She froze. She saw her life flash in front of her. She thought that she was going home to be with the Lord. The guy tried to shoot, but the gun didn't go off. The girls took off, and the guy disappeared, never to be seen again. Both Ana and Yolanda came home shaking like a leaf and told us what had just happened. Afterwards, Ana told me that although she was terrified having a gun pointed at her, she was also at peace, if God had determined it was her time to go to be with Him. She was ready to meet her maker.

Immediately I thought of the email I had received that morning. I shared how this lady in Sydney was awakened by the Lord last night to pray for us. At the time of her prayer, there wasn't any danger but all of a sudden there was a threat during the day. We believe that her obedience prevented this guy from shooting our Ana. Isn't it strange that God works this way? God is very capable of rescuing Ana Himself, but He chose someone far away to pray and intercede for that particular danger.

In the same way, God is quite capable of bringing the lost to Himself. He really doesn't need anyone to help Him, but He wants *us* to be involved. He wants us to go and make disciples of all nations. He wants us to understand His heartbeat, His passion, and His unconditional love for mankind. And as we work together with Him, we then shift our focus from ourselves to others. I believe that in this world we need to think less about ourselves and more about how we can reach out to others. To those who are so in need of a touch from the One who made us and

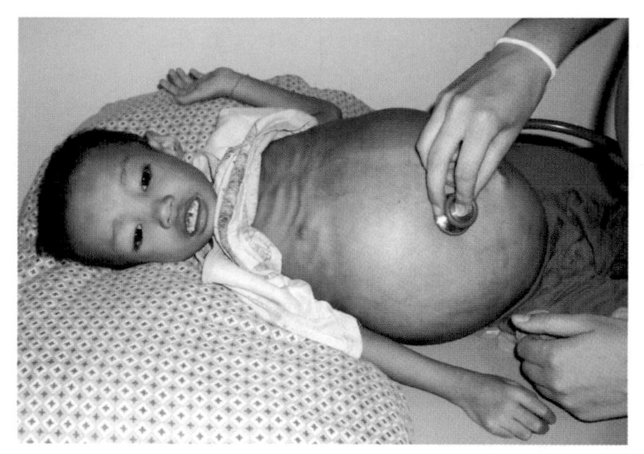

Little 3-year-old Tera was brought to us by her mother. She had already gone to several witchdoctors who failed to heal her. We had no idea what she had. Was it cancer, obstructed intestines, fluid? We had no proper medical equipment to diagnose her condition. We prayed for her, asking God to heal her, or take her home. That night, she died. We were all devastated, but we rejoiced that she was now with the Lord and no longer sick.

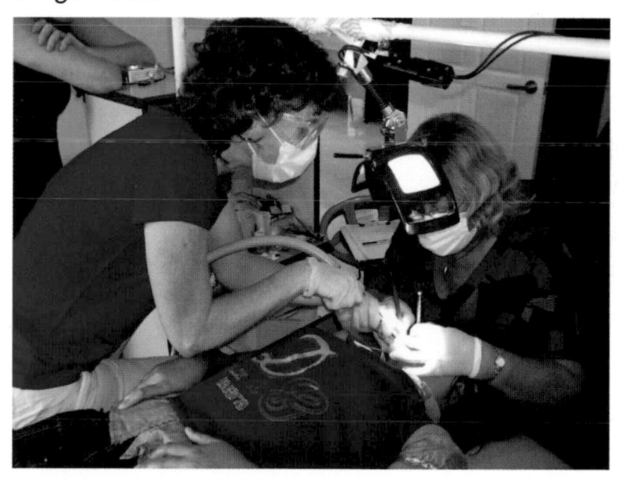

Kay and Lois (dentist from New Zealand), doing some dental work on one of our girls in our own dental clinic. Most of the children arriving at our home have terrible teeth from many years of poor diet.

understands us better than we could ever understand ourselves.

How I long to see the universal church, the body of Christ, stop arguing with each other about things that don't even matter to God, squandering valuable time and enormous resources on themselves, while people are dying everywhere. They must know that Jesus came and died for their sins, too. With the Holy Spirit's help, we should pool our God-given blessings of gifts, talents, and resources to go and make disciples of all families, all neighbourhoods, all villages, all towns, and all nations, baptizing them in the Name of the Father, and of the Son, and of the Holy Spirit. We must mirror Christ, wherever God takes us on our daily journey. We must share Jesus' love and salvation with a desperate world that is without hope and those who are willing to put their hope in any god who will have them. An impossible command? No. God wouldn't ask us to do something if He knew it weren't possible, or if He knew we couldn't do it. It *is* possible if we have faith. God desires us all to put His words into action. I tell you, if we truly understand that, this world would be a very different place.

So, how about you? Where are you with all this? Have you put God's words into action, or are you in the process of doing so? Are you waiting, thinking it should be left for someone else to do? Are you too busy with so many other things in life? The command to go and harvest souls is for all of us who put our trust in Him, not just for a select few. I challenge you, therefore, to make the most of every opportunity that He gives you every day. Be a mirror image of Jesus, a true and shining light in this world, empowered by the Holy Spirit. May people everywhere, from all walks of life, also want to seek and receive this King of Kings and Lord of Lords, Jesus Christ, into their lives because of what they see in our lives. What greater joy and sense of fulfillment is there than to know that God Almighty has used you in some way to help another soul come into His Kingdom. Pretty awesome, if you ask me. All glory to Him!

Find Out More….

If you would like to know more about Ronny and Kay Heyboer or Rivers of Life Ministries / Living Waters Village, visit us at www.heyboer.org or www.livingwatersvillage.com. Here you will also find information about receiving our newsletter.

If you have been inspired by reading this book or have any questions, please let us know by emailing ronnyheyboer@gmail.com or send a message to:

Ronny & Kay Heyboer
c/o Rivers of Life Ministries Borneo
P.O. Box 3203
93762 Kuching, Sarawak
Malaysia
(We receive our mail in Malaysia, although we live in Indonesia. Kuching, which is the capital city of Sarawak, Malaysia, is a 12-hour journey away. We pick up the mail regularly when one of our team members goes there.)

There are various ways to support the work in the jungle of Borneo through prayer, sponsoring a child, sending a donation, or coming over to help. Please go to our website for information.

Appendix A

Borneo Facts

Island: Borneo is the world's third largest island, mostly covered with mountains and dense rain forest. Its highest peak is Mount Kinabalu in Sabah, Malaysia, with an elevation of 4,101 m (13,455 ft.) above sea level.

Area: 743,330 km² (287,000 square miles), about twice the size of Germany.

Geography: Borneo is divided between Indonesia, Malaysia and Brunei. Indonesian Borneo, in the south, is called Kalimantan. Malaysian Borneo, in the north, is called East Malaysia. The sultanate of Brunei lies in northern Borneo. Nearly three-fourths of Borneo's population is in Kalimantan. Locals rarely use the term, "Borneo." The name originates from its Dutch colonial period.

Living Waters Village History

Location: West Kalimantan, in the Indonesian part of Borneo.

History: In 1995, Ronny and Kay Heyboer left Australia for Borneo. They began their work in the city of Kuching, East Malaysia, where Ronny was assisting with a local ministry's church planting program.

In 1997, they relocated to the Indonesian part of Borneo, West Kalimantan, where they continue to minister today.

Living Waters Village began in 2003, after God gave Ronny a vision to build a place to accommodate up to 1,000 impoverished, sick, abandoned, or orphaned children in the middle of the jungle and build schools for 2,000 children.

The Need: With an estimated 2014 population of more than 251 million people in Indonesia, it is difficult for many children here to attend school. First, there just aren't enough schools. Children in remote areas often have to leave their home to receive an education in a larger town or village. Second, children who do manage to attend school have other challenges: Children younger than 12 are often responsible for looking after younger brothers and sisters. In addition, they need to find work to pay for food, board, and school fees. Many children are malnourished, abused, and suffer from diseases such as tuberculosis, malaria and typhoid.

Statistics from Britannica.com and CIA World Factbook

Appendix B

Map of Borneo

Illustration from Google Maps